NEW DIRECTIONS FOR COMMUNITY COLLEGES

Arthur M. Cohen
EDITOR-IN-CHIEF

Florence B. Brawer
ASSOCIATE EDITOR

Building a Working Policy for Distance Education

Connie L. Dillon
University of Oklahoma

Rosa Cintrón
University of Oklahoma

EDITORS

Number 99, Fall 1997

JOSSEY-BASS PUBLISHERS
San Francisco

ERIC®

Clearinghouse for Community Colleges

BUILDING A WORKING POLICY FOR DISTANCE EDUCATION
Connie L. Dillon, Rosa Cintrón (eds.)
New Directions for Community Colleges, no. 99
Volume XXV, number 3
Arthur M. Cohen, Editor-in-Chief
Florence B. Brawer, Associate Editor

New Directions for Community Colleges is indexed in Current Index to Journals in Education (ERIC).

Microfilm copies of issues and articles are available in 16mm and 35mm, as well as microfiche in 105mm, through University Microfilms Inc., 300 North Zeeb Road, Ann Arbor, Michigan 48106-1346.

ISSN 0194-3081   ISBN 0-7879-9842-7

NEW DIRECTIONS FOR COMMUNITY COLLEGES is part of The Jossey-Bass Higher and Adult Education Series and is published quarterly by Jossey-Bass Inc., Publishers, 350 Sansome Street, San Francisco, California 94104-1342, in association with the ERIC Clearinghouse for Community Colleges. Periodicals postage paid at San Francisco, California, and at additional mailing offices. POSTMASTER: Send address changes to New Directions for Community Colleges, Jossey-Bass Inc., Publishers, 350 Sansome Street, San Francisco, California 94104-1342.

SUBSCRIPTIONS cost $55.00 for individuals and $98.00 for institutions, agencies, and libraries. Prices subject to change.

THE MATERIAL in this publication is based on work sponsored wholly or in part by the Office of Educational Research and Improvement, U.S. Department of Education, under contract number RI-93-00-2003. Its contents do not necessarily reflect the views of the Department or any other agency of the U.S. Government.

EDITORIAL CORRESPONDENCE should be sent to the Editor-in-Chief, Arthur M. Cohen, at the ERIC Clearinghouse for Community Colleges, University of California, 3051 Moore Hall, 405 Hilgard Avenue, Los Angeles, California 90024-1521.

Cover photograph © Rene Sheret, After Image, Los Angeles, California, 1990.

Jossey-Bass Web address: http://www.josseybass.com

Printed in the United States of America on acid-free recycled paper containing 100 percent recovered waste paper, of which at least 20 percent is postconsumer waste.

CONTENTS

To our daughters, Jenny and Sara

EDITORS' NOTES

The place of postsecondary education in twenty-first-century education depends upon its ability to harness the power of technology to offer educational opportunity without the constraints of time, distance, or individual differences. However, despite a considerable body of research attesting to its effectiveness, distance education lingers on the periphery of higher education practice. We have come to realize that the adoption of distance education in higher education depends not upon a rational system that eagerly embraces the latest research, but rather upon a political system designed to mediate among many competing values. The failure to integrate distance education is not a failure of research, but rather a function of the combined effects of federal, state, and institutional policies that discourage educational change. Institutional reward structures promote convention rather than innovation. State policies fund teaching rather than learning, and federal policies fund credits rather than outcomes. Thus issues of policy rather than issues of effectiveness will ultimately determine the place of distance education in higher education.

The question we must ask today is not whether we can afford to use telecommunications in higher education, but rather whether we can afford not to. For unlike past developments, the revolutionary change promised by technology is not a change emanating from within higher education; it is a change from outside. The name of that change is competition—competition from educational providers unfettered by state regulation, costly infrastructure, or geography who can tap into our faculty, our libraries, and our authority to credential (Goldstein, 1993).

The community college is an appropriate focus for this book because, if predictions of fundamental change come true, it will be the community college that will define that change. Emerging early in the twentieth century as a response to the demands of an increasingly literate society, the community college thrives on change. Historically, community colleges have had "no traditions to defend, no alumni to question their role, no autonomous professional staff to be moved aside, no statements of philosophy that would militate against taking on responsibilities for everything" (Cohen and Brawer, 1996, pp. 2–3).

The open-door mission brought to the community college students with diverse interests, needs, and abilities. This diversity fostered a climate of innovation, a faculty focused singularly upon teaching, and a responsiveness to instructional technology unique within public education (Cohen and Brawer, 1996). It is the community college that has embraced classroom computer technology, using computer-based labs and classrooms at nearly twice the rate of public universities. Likewise, it is the community college that has demonstrated the greatest use of and commitment to the application of the distance education technologies (Lever-Duffy and Lemke, 1996; Brey, 1991). If distance education requires us to transform our vision of teaching and learning, that vision will be largely defined by the community college.

This volume is composed of a series of chapters that address the policy implications of distance education for the community college. The chapters include case studies, research, and literature reviews designed to provide practical and generalizable responses to the emerging telecommunications environment by states, regions, and institutions.

In Chapter One, Arlene Parisot discusses the impact of distance education upon faculty. She reports the findings of a study that examined the teaching styles of community college faculty and explores the institutional factors that influence the change in teaching distance education requires. In Chapter Two, Douglas Lape and Patricia Hart report findings from a study of attitudes toward distance education, and suggest that differences among leadership groups must be addressed if educators are to make optimal use of distance education in the community college. In Chapter Three, Patricia Kovel-Jarboe uses a study of state system policy development in Minnesota to explore the role of the community college in state system planning.

In Chapter Four, Suzanna Spears and Randy Tatroe discuss the role of state policy in encouraging the development of partnerships between community colleges, rural schools, and telecommunications providers. This chapter is a case study of the development of one such partnership in the state of Colorado. In Chapter Five, Patrick Dallet and John Opper present a case study describing Florida's plans to use distance education at the community college to meet increased demands with fewer resources. They discuss how fundamental changes in views of teaching and learning require fundamental changes in approaches to conceptualizing education.

In Chapter Six, Christine Sorensen describes the criteria used to evaluate distance education in Iowa and how the community college can serve as an advocate of local needs in a system that is increasingly defined by state, multistate, and national issues. In Chapter Seven, Sally Johnstone and Stephen Tilson describe the concept of the virtual university, provide an example of the development of one such university—the Western Governors University (WGU)—and discuss the implications for the community college. In Chapter Eight, Barbara Gellman-Danley summarizes the findings of a research study designed to examine how the regional accrediting associations are addressing quality assurance in the age of distributed learning. Chapter Nine, by Marina McIsaac and Jeremy Rowe, explores the impact of the tension between the constitutional right to property from which current copyright policy has evolved and the culture of intellectual sharing that dominates higher education practice. They summarize the current status of federal copyright law and provide a summary of principles institutions can use to guide the development of institutional copyright policies. Finally, in Chapter Ten the editors review the current research on distance education and the community college and explore today's answers from the perspective of tomorrow's questions.

Connie L. Dillon
Rosa Cintrón
Editors

References

Brey, R. *U.S. Postsecondary Distance Learning Programs in the 1990s: A Decade of Growth.* (Report No. JC 920 023). Washington, D.C.: Instructional Telecommunications Consortium, American Association of Community and Junior Colleges, 1991. (ED 340 418)

Cohen, A., and Brawer, F. *The American Community College.* (3rd ed.) San Francisco: Jossey-Bass, 1996.

Goldstein, M. B. "Technology and the Law: What Every Community College Leader Needs to Know." *AACC Journal,* 1993, *64* (3), 31–36.

Lever-Duffy, J., and Lemke, R. A. *Learning Without Limits: Model Distance Education Programs in Community Colleges.* Mission Viejo, Calif.: League for Innovation, 1996.

CONNIE L. DILLON is an associate professor of adult and higher education at the University of Oklahoma, where she specializes in the study of distance education and telecommunications.

ROSA CINTRÓN is an assistant professor of adult and higher education at the University of Oklahoma. She specializes in the study of student personnel services and the American community college.

This chapter examines the variables that affect the adoption or rejection of distance education by community college faculty and proposes a model to support changes in faculty roles required by the adoption of technology.

Distance Education as a Catalyst for Changing Teaching in the Community College: Implications for Institutional Policy

Arlene H. Parisot

Change is the most pervasive force in current postsecondary educational institutions. In this environment, community colleges view themselves as a cost-effective alternative in providing the education and training necessary to enter today's technology-driven job market. Even though community colleges are "grappling with eroding budgets, demographic shifts, and diversity," it is time to "get serious about technology's role on campuses—its place in relation to curricula and how it will impact those who learn" (Phelps, 1994, p. 25).

Faculty are crucial to implementation of any new technological change. However, little has been done to understand the changing role of faculty in adapting to technology and the changes in the psychological and physical environment promised by distance learning. Therefore, a more thorough understanding of the faculty experience in the distance learning environment is important to the formulation of institutional policies designed to guide the diffusion of distance learning into the teaching process.

This chapter describes the results of a qualitative case study (Parisot, 1995) designed to shed light on the factors that influence faculty decisions relative to the adoption of distance learning technologies and ultimately the factors that influence changes in teaching style. The findings of this study led to the development of a conceptual framework for consensus building, a model that can be used to link the development of institutional policy to the changing role of faculty in the distance learning environment. The consensus-building model is designed to guide community colleges as they seek to reframe institutional policies for the distance learning environment.

The Structure of the Study

The study was designed to assess the teaching styles of faculty, current faculty use of technology, and the factors that influence the acceptance or rejection of distance technologies. The population of the study were faculty of a public community college. A purposeful sample (Patton, 1987) of twenty-seven participants was identified from a roster of one hundred faculty members. The sample was selected to include a variety of disciplines, gender diversity, and both full-time faculty and faculty who held joint administrative positions.

Data were collected using both qualitative and quantitative methods. All participants were interviewed to assess their current use of technology, their perceptions of the impact of technology on their teaching and student learning, and the factors that encouraged or discouraged their use of technology. Interview data were analyzed using qualitative content analysis techniques to identify themes. Quantitative data were collected using the Principles of Adult Learning Scale (PALS), an instrument designed to assess preferences for teacher-centered or student-centered approaches to teaching (Conti, 1985). The overall PALS score can range from 0 to 220. The mean for the instrument is 146 with a standard deviation of 20. High scores represent a preference for student-centered approaches, in which the decisions of content and methods are shared by teachers and learners; and low scores represent a preference for teacher-centered approaches, in which the teacher assumes the primary authority for the class structure.

Findings

The Principles of Adult Learning Style instrument was completed by twenty (74 percent) of the participating faculty. The analysis of these data indicated a strong teacher-centered orientation. The scores ranged from 91 to 176 with a group mean of 123.48, which is 1.1 standard deviation below the mean for the instrument.

The interviews produced a qualitative description of the community college as a changing institution, with diffusion of technology described as occurring within specific departments rather than across the institution as a whole. Technology was viewed primarily as an enhancement of teaching rather than a vehicle for changing the ways of teaching. Faculty expressed concerns about the benefit to students and learning. The interviews revealed a range of opinions regarding the impact of technology on the role of the teacher in the classroom. Some saw it as a challenge to be met while others viewed it as a threat.

The faculty identified three major factors that would encourage the use of technology: role modeling, faculty involvement, and support. Role modeling was a primary motivational factor in the adoption and diffusion of technology.

Opinion leaders, those individuals who were able to influence others' attitudes over behavior (Rogers, 1983), were of importance to this process of behavior change. From the faculty perspective, being a decision maker in the process of developing and implementing a technology plan assured relevancy of the technology to the task and reduced fear of loss of authority or position. Issues of concern included convenient access to equipment, timely training programs, availability of technical expertise and administrative support, and appropriate incentives.

Barriers to embracing the use of technology as an instructional tool centered on the investment of time needed to develop new programs, as well as on attitudinal factors. Many faculty felt intimidated by technology and were concerned about a loss of control and comfort with standard practices.

The findings of this study are compatible with Rogers's diffusion of innovation theory (1983). Rogers identifies five characteristics of innovation that can explain the rate of adoption. These are complexity, compatibility, observability, trialability, and perceived relative advantage. According to the faculty interviewed for this study, the technology needs to be easy to use. It must be consistent with existing values, and there needs to be a real value beyond use of technology for its own sake. Faculty must also be able to try it, they need to observe others using it, and they must view it as better than what they have now. Faculty also tend to be teacher-centered in their approach to teaching and tend to view technology as an aid to support current teacher-centered strategies rather than as a vehicle for changing approaches to teaching.

Discussion

The results of this study provided insight into the process needed to design institutional policies that will encourage the use of technology. Based on the findings, a conceptual framework for consensus building was developed. The framework encompasses four areas: first, *acknowledgment* provides recognition of the need to change and is used to create a shared vision. *Awareness* is fostered during the knowledge- and agreement-building process, in which the potential impact of technology is examined and debated. Third, *acculturation* guides new ways of thinking about teaching and learning. Finally, *affirmation* represents the value-building process in which the faculty make a commitment to participate in the adoption of technological innovation. This conceptual framework serves as the guide for developing an institutional blueprint of policy formation for distance education.

Acknowledgment: The Vision-Building Process. *Acknowledgment* of the need for change by all segments of the institution is an important first step toward establishing a philosophical base supporting changes in policy. Institutionwide involvement is imperative for building such a vision and faculty are pivotal in that they must become stakeholders and assume a sense of ownership for the process of integrating technology into the educational delivery system. As one faculty-administrator interviewed in this study stated, "I think that it is important that faculty have the kind of technology they ask for rather than hearing there is this new thing out there, you ought to be using it. When it comes from without, it is not as encouraging as it would be if we were to have a real need for this. There should be a real give and take. Real faculty involvement is a must" (Parisot, 1995, p. 100). Another faculty member of this community college said, "I want to have more input into what is going on. I am afraid that decisions are made without us being involved. I am afraid we are going to lose jobs and things like that" (p. 100).

Awareness: The Knowledge- and Agreement-Building Process. Rogers's (1983) model of the innovation-decision process begins with the Knowledge Stage, when the individual (or unit) is made aware of the innovation and gains some understanding of its function. During this phase, the information that is sought is of three types: software information (what the innovation is and how it works), how-to knowledge (techniques needed to use an innovation properly), and principles knowledge (the underlying principles of how the innovation works) (Rogers, 1983, p. 167). With knowledge of the innovation, the individual (or unit) moves toward the Persuasion Stage and forms a favorable or unfavorable attitude toward the innovation. It is at this point that the attitude toward the innovation is affective rather than cognitive, and the individual questions personal consequences and impact.

In opposition to Rogers's model of a process by which decisions are reached in regard to adoption of an innovation, the standard approach that educational institutions have initiated to integrate complex instructional technologies into the classroom has been to buy these technologies and simply make them available. From this view, "there is little more to be done except to let teachers get on with practicing their craft as they have always done" (Moore, 1993, p. 1).

In the real world, however, the "attitudinal issues—how people perceive and react to these technologies—are far more important now than structural and technical obstacles in influencing the use of technology in higher education" (McNeil, 1990, p. 2). Technology is viewed as a force to be tamed. Attitudinal issues such as intimidation, resistance to change, and loss of comfort zone do much to discourage the use of technology. This is shown by the response of a computer information systems instructor: "The problem is continuing to glorify technology; continuing to see it as something other than just another tool. If people see it as just another tool, that is good because they can approach it as you would a piece of paper. If they approach it as this larger than life thing, then they would be intimidated by it" (Parisot, 1995, p. 103). From the viewpoint of one computer science faculty member, resistance to using technology may just be a matter of fear and the result of "a phenomenon called cyberphobia or fear of technology" (p. 103).

Building *awareness* and knowledge can be accomplished by incorporating Rogers's components of trialability, relative advantage, and compatibility into the process. For adoption of technological innovation to occur, there must be opportunities to experiment with the technology. A language instructor saw a need to see how it works. "I am like a student, I need to be exposed to good stuff" (Parisot, 1995, p. 104). A nursing administrator believed that "Once they got hooked on it, you can't stop them" (p. 105). Also there is a need to understand the relative advantage of using technology. A computer information systems faculty member stated, "Why I don't use it in the classroom is because I haven't seen where it is giving me some big advantage over just writing on the board and no one has shown me why it is better" (p. 105). It must be consistent with existing values: "Changing for change's sake is not worth it. There has to be a real value that goes beyond technology" (p. 115).

Acculturation: The Decision-Building Process. *Acculturation*—the process of adopting the traits and patterns of a new way of teaching and learning—can only be successful when the underlying philosophy for the process recognizes that "people will act in terms of what they perceive to be available to them in any given situation; that is they will act in terms of what they perceive as possible" (Maehr and Braskamp, 1986, p. 40). Also the option needs to be perceived as acceptable and tied in with what is right and proper—judgments that are based in large part on one's membership in particular sociocultural groups and the roles one plays. Emphasis on cognition in understanding motivation underscores the importance of internal thoughts regarding the self as well as the situation in encouraging a positive attitude toward a new learning experience (Parisot, 1995).

When examining the motivational components necessary for the teacher as an adult learner to engage in situations that require change, it is important to analyze the thoughts that the individual constructs regarding the self and the situation. Thoughts about self center on the judgment of significant others, feelings of self-confidence, and self-determination. Thoughts about the situation focus on whether it is considered a viable option and whether it is acceptable in relation to the individual's value system and the social environment in which the situation would occur. As an example, if thoughts regarding the teacher's role in the classroom and the nature of the learner are based on traditional pedagogy, then—as one arts administrator who was also a faculty member believed—using innovative technology might require relinquishing the power that being the provider of information affords. To be a facilitator requires faculty to move from a teacher-centered role into a learner-centered role. "I think that fear comes from some people's inability to relinquish the personal power that is information. As technology becomes more accessible, it will democratize education from the student's point of view. Faculty have to see themselves as the facilitator not a storer" (Parisot, 1995, p. 97).

Technology-based instruction is essentially mediated instruction, therefore the technology is interposed between student and teacher and between student and student (Florini, 1989, p. 49). Teachers will need to collaborate with technicians and program developers, which could affect a teacher's perception of autonomy and teaching style. An arts and humanities administrator identified as having a learner-centered orientation to the delivery of instruction had relevant advice for others: "Maybe we ought not to be lecturing, ought not to be using the technology to make an outmoded pedagogical medium like lecture to be attractive. This concerns me. The students are sitting there and instead of passively listening to an instructor and taking notes, they are passively watching a presentation and taking notes. If we are not careful, technology is going to take us forward into the 19th century rather than forward to the 21st century" (Parisot, 1995, p. 96).

An arts and humanities faculty member was also prepared to actively engage in change: "If I can be replaced in the classroom, it will take place and should take place. Perhaps what that will do will be to free me up to be more creative in other ways and take on new roles in the classroom that I couldn't take on before. I welcome having some of the drudgery taken away . . . anything you can do to make me more efficient, then do it" (p. 95).

This study found evidence of a willingness to look at alternatives to teacher-centered approaches. In reference to the PALS instrument itself, one faculty member commented: "Some (many really) of the questions are causing me to review my methods" (p. 117).

Developing an awareness of teaching style and the philosophical foundation upon which it is shaped could allow for development of "a personally constructed model to help teachers make effective instructional use of technology without sacrificing important aspects of their teaching style" (Florini, 1989, p. 51). Being able to evaluate the compatibility of one's teaching style with technology as a delivery mechanism would foster adoption and diffusion of technology across the instructional environment. It might also provide the stimulus for making a paradigm shift from a teacher-centered to a learner-centered style. One faculty member expressed a desire to make this transition in exactly those words—"I want to get away from teacher-centered and evolve toward learner-centered" (Parisot, 1995, p. 117).

In moving faculty toward a decision to adopt technology, role modeling or peer observation is a primary motivational factor. Rogers's innovation-decision process defines the Decision Stage as occurring when the individual (or unit) takes steps toward making a choice to adopt or reject the innovation. Most individuals do not adopt an innovation without trying it first, though some individuals will accept trial by a peer as a substitute for a personal trial of the innovation prior to adoption (Rogers, 1983). A computer science instructor said, "I need to see success. I like to see other instructors trying something. I would be more encouraged by seeing a peer develop it." (Parisot, 1995, p. 99). An arts and humanities faculty member simply said, "I need a role model" (p. 99). Opportunities for faculty to observe and interact with peers who successfully employ technology are a major motivational factor in encouraging use of technology.

To achieve acculturation, the process of adopting the traits and patterns of a new way of teaching and learning, the individual must be able to perceive that it is possible and that it has value within the immediate sociocultural group. Acculturation is the decision-building process. As such, it promotes examination of the teaching-learning transaction and the philosophical foundation upon which it is based to encourage building a teaching model compatible with technology. Institutional policy that promotes faculty acceptance of technology as an instructional tool must give consideration to the components necessary for the teacher as an adult learner to engage in situations that require change.

Affirmation: The Value-Building Process. Affirmation of an action or belief requires positive declaration. Affirming the decision by faculty to participate in the adoption of technological innovation, with its accompanying potential for changing the teaching and learning process, requires the institution to recognize the value and worth of that decision.

Rogers's Implementation Stage is the point at which an individual (or unit) puts an innovation into use. This stage implies overt behavior as the new idea is implemented. This stage is important in that it is one thing for adoption to occur but quite another to actually use the innovation. The questions asked during this phase relate to access, use, and overcoming problems associated with use. It is at this time that support is necessary for success. Provision of timely faculty development programs, accessible equipment, available technical expertise, and appropriate incentives gives institutional value and worth to the decision by faculty to integrate technology into the instructional environment. One community college administrator understands what can encourage use of instructional innovation: "If you are looking at encouraging faculty to use technology, you have to provide training and release time. You can't just say here it is, now go back to the classroom and use it. You have to give some type of release time, some type of reward, some type of training so they can produce something and they can see some type of benefit for themselves" (Parisot, 1995, p. 101).

Support as a motivational factor also means reevaluating the needs that new technologies engender. As a mathematics faculty member stressed, "We have to change the way we think about equipping instructors. Right now we have to use professional development dollars to upgrade. If I am interested in a piece of software and am willing to put in the time to learn it, they should hand it to me. I realize it is expensive, but we have to make it easy. It is a question of accessibility and support" (Parisot, p. 100).

The Implementation Stage ends when the innovation becomes institutionalized. The Confirmation Stage is the terminal stage in the innovation-decision process, when individuals seek reinforcement for the innovation decision already made, but run the risk of reversing the decision if conflicting information about the innovation is received. The adopter seeks to reduce dissonance but will react to information that leads to questioning the merit of the innovation. At this point the adopter may possibly discontinue use of the innovation (Rogers, 1983).

Dissonance may occur if the institution, in its management of faculty, does not recognize, reward, and support those willing to invest time and creativity to use technology as an instructional tool equally with those practicing traditional teaching. Faculty are encouraged "if the cost of support for the technology is built in up front" and "if there is commitment from administration that money will be available to maintain the equipment" (Parisot, 1995, p. 120). Affirmation as the value-building process requires positive declaration through policy to ensure institutionalization and continued use of technology within the instructional environment.

A Blueprint for Policy

Within this environment of change, institutions need to address the barriers that impede the adoption and use of distance technologies by faculty and build policy that encourages openness to new teaching methods, as well as changes in a college's organizational and administrative structure. In what manner and to what extent faculty will use technology as an instructional tool will be determined in large part by the leadership provided through institutional policy. The conceptual framework for consensus building presented in this chapter is a guide for institutions to define policy within an environment of change.

Acknowledgment of the need for change, the vision-building process, is the first step toward achieving consensus. All segments of the campus must be included in the development and implementation of a technology plan for an educational institution to assure shared ownership and responsibility for the stated outcomes of a coordinated plan.

Awareness guides the knowledge and agreement-building process, and is enhanced when faculty receive comprehensive training in the use of specific technologies, as well as access to current research or successful practices relating to technology and student learning outcomes. Such training and knowledge will do much to overcome the attitudinal barriers that discourage use of technology.

Acculturation to new ways of teaching and learning, the decision-building process, is realized through providing opportunities for professional development and peer role modeling. Professional development needs to be designed to allow faculty to examine teaching styles and the philosophical foundations upon which they are based.

Peer role modeling suggests that trained faculty will in turn become the role models for others and the interpersonal communication channels that serve to influence the decision of members of their social system to adopt the innovation. Institutions should identify faculty members who are considered opinion leaders—individuals able to influence other individuals' attitudes or overt behavior in a desired way (Rogers, 1983, p. 248).

Affirmation of the commitment to participate in the adoption of technological innovation, the value-building process, is solidified through development of academic policies that focus on the management of faculty. Creating a team approach to the design of courses integrating technology, providing release time for faculty to participate in the design of new models of teaching, initiating discussion roundtables focusing on teaching, learning, and technology, and recognizing and rewarding faculty innovators in the design and delivery of courses through technology will do much to convey the value that institutions place on the commitment by faculty to engage in using technology as an instructional tool.

The growth of technology in education will place demands on institutions to provide an infrastructure that encourages faculty acceptance and continued use of technology as a viable instructional tool. Faculty acceptance will be the key to successful integration of technology into the teaching and learning process. Faculty acceptance will not occur in an institutional vacuum. Institutions must begin to reassess policies designed for traditional classroom teacher-centered approaches to learning and develop policies that address the capabilities that the new technologies have for meeting the needs of the twenty-first-century learning environment.

References

Conti, G. "Assessing Teaching Style in Adult Education: How and Why." *Lifelong Learning,* 1985, *8* (8), 7–11.

Florini, B. M. "Teaching Styles And Technology." In E. Hayes (ed.), *Effective Teaching Styles.* New Directions for Continuing Education, no. 43. San Francisco: Jossey-Bass, 1989.

Maehr, M. L., and Braskamp, L. A. *The Motivation Factor: A Theory of Personal Investment.* San Francisco: New Lexington Press, 1986.

McNeil, D. R. "Wiring the Ivory Tower: A Round Table on Technology in Higher Education." In D. Steward and J. S. Daniel (eds.), *Proceedings of the International Council for Distance Education.* Oslo, Norway: International Council for Distance Education, 1990.

Moore, M. G. "Is Teaching Like Flying? A Total Systems View of Distance Education." *American Journal of Distance Education,* 1993, *7* (1), 1–10.

Parisot, A. H. "Technology and Teaching: The Adoption and Diffusion of Technological Innovations by a Community College Faculty." Unpublished doctoral dissertation, Montana State University, Bozeman, 1995.

Patton, M. Q. *How to Use Qualitative Methods in Evaluation.* Thousand Oaks, Calif.: Sage, 1987.

Phelps, D. G. "What Lies Ahead for Community Colleges as We Hurtle Toward the 21st Century?" *Community College Journal,* 1994, *1,* 22–35.

Rogers, E. M. *Diffusion of Innovations.* (3rd ed.) New York: Free Press, 1983.

ARLENE H. PARISOT is currently distance education director and chair of student services at Montana State College of Technology–Great Falls, where she works in the area of faculty development for distance education.

This chapter describes a study that examines differences in levels of awareness of distance education among key community college leadership groups.

Changing the Way We Teach by Changing the College: Leading the Way Together

Douglas H. Lape, Patricia K. Hart

Community colleges are expected to meet the changing needs of the communities they serve through open access, a high-quality and diverse curriculum, and an array of alternative delivery systems that accommodate increasingly complex student lifestyles. But distance education requires fundamental changes in traditional approaches to education, changes that require both understanding and acceptance of the possibilities distance technologies offer. Verduin and Clark (1991) report that administrators and faculty who use distance education feel confident about the methodology and request its use. Conversely, educators with little awareness or understanding about distance education systems tend to question its viability and effectiveness.

Distance education requires the reconceptualization of institutional policies. If policy is the vehicle institutions use to realize their goals, then leadership is the ability to unite the people in an organization toward a common goal (Uveges, 1971). Changing institutional policy to realize the goal of individualized, student-centered learning promised by distance education requires the support of all community college leadership groups. Before institutional policies can be changed, we must determine what our leaders know about distance education, the importance they place on distance education methods, and whether or not differences exist among the various leadership groups. This study assesses the level of awareness and understanding of distance education of key community college leaders and differences within key leadership groups.

The Structure of the Study

The population of the study is selected leaders from the twenty-nine community colleges in the state of Michigan. The five leadership groups identified are the president, the chief financial officer, the dean of liberal studies, the chair of the social science division (as a representative of the faculty), and the media service director.

These five groups were identified as representative of the key leadership positions in the community college system for the following reasons. The support of the president is an important factor in the success or failure of an innovation, since it is the president, working with the board of trustees, who recommends policies and procedures that provide the framework for program development for the college. The support of the chief financial officer is critical because the implementation of distance education requires a considerable investment in infrastructure and capital. The dean of liberal studies was selected as representative of the chief academic officers based upon the assumption that these deans would be more conservative in their acceptance of technology than deans of occupational programs. The chair of the social science division was selected as most representative of faculty because social sciences is a requirement for most degree programs. In addition, research indicates that the support or resistance of department chairs and division directors is an important variable in instructional change (Kozma, 1985; Tucker and Bryan, 1989). The media service directors and their staff provide the technical expertise, equipment support, and training required to implement innovative distance education technology.

Participants in the study received a mailed questionnaire consisting of items with discrete closed responses (yes, no, I don't know), items with continuous Likert scale responses (1 to 5 scales ranging from strongly agree to disagree), and one open response item. The survey items were identified based on a review of the literature concerning the factors that need to be considered when building support for the implementation of distance education: planning, curricula, and cost (Levine, 1992; Clark, 1993; Bunting, 1989; Dillon, 1989; Kozma, 1985).

Analysis of variance, using the SPSS statistical data analysis software, was used to determine if the means of the leadership groups were equal. Post hoc multiple comparison procedures were used to determine which pairs of groups appeared to have different means. Differences in the pairs of means were identified using the least-significant difference (LSD) test.

A total of 145 surveys were distributed to the five leadership groups at the twenty-nine community colleges in the state of Michigan. Survey responses were received from twenty-seven of the twenty-nine community colleges—116 individual responses, a response rate of 80 percent. The return rates for the five leadership groups ranged from 68.9 percent (n = 20) for the finance officers to 93.1 percent (n = 27) for the deans. The remaining three groups—presidents, media directors, and chairs—each had return rates of 79.3 percent (n = 23). At least one of the respondents from twenty-five of the colleges was aware of distance education activities at that college. (All of the responding colleges do employ at least one distance education delivery system.)

Findings

The study findings are organized according to three predominant themes in the literature: planning, curricular issues, and cost-effectiveness in distance education. Planning includes needs assessment, policy barriers, and evaluation. Curricular concerns focus on the quality of the distance learning experience. Finally, cost-effectiveness and efficiency are factors in the selection of models to be used to assess the relative costs and benefits of distance education.

Planning for Distance Education. An important first step in planning is to determine if a need exists (Duning, Van Kekerix, and Zaborowski, 1993). Although the findings of this study indicate that most respondents believe there is a need for distance education at their college, a majority did not base this belief on any known market analysis or supporting information.

Compatibility with institutional mission is necessary for successful distance education (Levine, 1992). When asked about the compatibility between the college mission statement and distance education, 89.7 percent of the respondents were positive. However, differences among the five leadership groups were significant at the 0.05 alpha level. Further analysis found that the means for the faculty were substantially different when compared to the means of the other four groups, with 30.4 percent of the chairs responding more negatively with regard to mission compatibility.

When asked if there were any policies or regulations that might serve as barriers to the success of distance education programs at their college, 32.8 percent responded positively. The most predominant barriers identified related to employment contracts (13.8 percent) and funding and tuition (5 percent each).

When asked if distance education courses should be evaluated differently from traditional courses, over one-third of the respondents (38.8 percent) responded affirmatively, while another 38.8 percent felt these courses should not be evaluated differently.

Curricular Issues in Distance Education. The responses indicated that the majority of survey participants felt that distance students performed as well as traditional students, a finding compatible with research. However, an analysis of variance identified significant differences among the leadership groups at the 0.05 alpha level. Further analysis found that the means for the chairs were substantially different, with chairs indicating the greater skepticism in the academic performance of distance students, and the greatest differences in means between the faculty and the deans.

The respondents agreed with the literature suggesting that distance education requires changes in teaching and in the presentation of content (Beaudoin, 1990; Verduin and Clark, 1991), with 95.7 percent of the respondents agreeing that distance education would change teaching practices of faculty.

Some research indicates that distance education limits the interaction between faculty and students (Markwood and Johnstone, 1992). Over 40 percent of the respondents felt that interaction would be limited in a distance setting, while 37 percent disagreed or strongly disagreed, and the remaining 18.1 percent were neutral or had no opinion.

With respect to the quality of nationally marketed, prepackaged courses, 42.3 percent of the respondents indicated that these courses are equal to courses prepared by campus faculty, and 20.7 percent disagreed. The remaining 33.6 percent were neutral or had no opinion. However, an analysis of variance found significant differences between the leadership groups on this item and further analysis found significant differences in the responses of chairs and deans. More chairs than deans felt that courses prepared by faculty were better in quality than prepackaged courses.

Survey responses were in agreement with the findings of a study by Dillon (1989), which found that distance education requires incentives for faculty participation, with 75.9 percent responding positively to this statement. Regarding the need for additional preparation and planning time for distance education courses, the majority of survey respondents (74.1 percent) indicated that faculty who taught distance courses needed additional time, and 12.1 percent disagreed.

Cost-Effectiveness and Efficiency of Distance Education. Relating the educational benefits of a course or program to the cost-effectiveness of delivering that course or program to remote sites is one of the key concerns with distance education, but one difficult to assess (Rumble, 1986). The cost-effectiveness of distance education requires an examination of the effectiveness of decision alternatives. When assessing the cost-effectiveness of distance education it is important to realize that placing a value on benefits to the various stakeholders is difficult (Ansari, 1992).

Although using telecommunications for distance delivery of courses is assumed to be expensive, the reality is that the costs range widely depending upon the technology used and the design of the system (Mace, 1982; Rumble, 1988; Levin, 1981; Levine, 1992; Duning, Van Kekerix, and Zaborowski, 1993). Some of the models used to assess the cost-effectiveness of distance education appear to address the costs of alternatives while ignoring the benefits. Other models assume that the benefits of the alternatives are equal (Mace, 1982; Duning, Van Kekerix, and Zaborowski, 1993; Hart, 1994).

Institutions planning to conduct cost and benefit studies will need to define the methods and model that will be best suited to their unique program goals and accepted by all leadership groups. The cost-effectiveness issues addressed in this study include whether distance education is cost-effective, whether both the costs and benefits of distance education courses should be considered, whether it is possible to compare costs of distance and traditional delivery, and finally whether the investment in distance education is a benefit to the faculty, staff, and students.

Regarding the cost-effectiveness of distance education, 75 percent of the respondents felt that distance education was cost-effective, compared to 6.9 percent who disagreed. In addition, the majority of respondents (92.3 percent) felt that both the costs and benefits of distance education should be computed to assess cost-effectiveness. To determine if the means of the leadership groups were equal, analysis of variance was employed. The differences in the population means between the five leadership groups and the survey questions were significant at the 0.05 alpha level. Further analysis found differences in the responses of the media service directors' group when compared to the remaining four groups, with 30.4 percent of the media service directors selecting a neutral response.

The majority of survey respondents (56 percent) disagreed with the statement that cost comparisons are useless due to differences in the cost structures of distance and traditional education. Concerning the benefit of distance education to faculty, staff, and students, 81.9 percent of the respondents indicated that distance education was beneficial. An analysis of variance found differences at the 0.05 alpha level between the five leadership groups regarding benefits of distance education. Further analysis found differences in the responses of chairs compared to the other four groups, with the chairs responding less favorably.

Conclusions

The findings of this study are important in two respects. The first is the identification of factors that may increase the likelihood of adopting distance education methods; and the second addresses factors that may impede the adoption of distance education.

The literature suggests that distance education will more likely be adopted if it is perceived to be compatible with the college mission, and perceived to be effective from both an academic and cost perspective. The results of this study found positive responses from the leadership groups with respect to all these factors, indicating in general that a positive climate exists for the adoption of distance education methods. In addition, all the leadership groups agreed that certain policies may serve as barriers to distance education, and all groups were able to identify potential barriers. A key factor in the acceptance of distance education is the recognition among leadership groups that changes in teaching patterns required by distance education must be accompanied by institutional incentives and support for planning and development of courses (Dillon, 1989; Levine, 1992; Duning, Van Kekerix, and Zaborowski, 1993). All the leadership groups surveyed in this study recognized this need. Once a need is recognized, accompanying changes in the incentive and support systems become increasingly likely.

The findings of this study are compatible with the literature with regard to whether cost-effectiveness studies can be done (Rumble, 1988; Levin, 1981; Duning, Van Kekerix, and Zaborowski, 1993) and with regard to the opinion that cost-effectiveness needs to consider both benefits and costs (Duning, Van Kekerix, and Zaborowski, 1993; Ansari, 1992). The majority of respondents believe that comparisons between distance and traditional education are possible, and a substantial number of the survey respondents believe that the investment in distance education systems is a benefit to the faculty, staff, and students. However, in contrast to findings of a study by Gunawardena (1990) that found those implementing distance education do not believe it always a cost-effective alternative to traditional education, the majority of respondents in this study believe that distance education is cost-effective. Community colleges need to address the desired benefits of distance education for faculty, staff, and students, and it is important to recognize that both the perceived benefits and strength of these benefits varies among the different groups.

Second, the study also identified potential barriers to the adoption of distance education. Although the majority of respondents believed that distance education is needed at their institution, there was little supporting market analysis data. The findings indicate that community college leaders have not documented a need for distance learning. Distance education often requires a considerable investment of resources. All too often colleges embrace a technology and then search for a need that fits the technology, rather than identifying a need and searching for the technology that fits the need. The practice of adopting technological solutions to perceived rather than real needs may result in an inefficient use of resources and a negative climate for innovation, a condition that makes the future of distance education somewhat precarious.

The findings of this study indicate that there are substantial differences between the chairs as representative of the faculty and the other four leadership groups concerning perceptions of the effectiveness of distance education, with the greatest differences identified between chairs and the deans. Chairs expressed more doubts about the compatibility of distance education with the institutional mission than the other leadership groups. The chairs responded less positively than the other groups to the potential benefits of distance education. In addition, the chairs were less likely to believe that distance education courses were educationally effective. Although much of the research has found that the amount of interaction between faculty and students is increased through distance education (Brey, 1991; Moore, 1990; Markwood and Johnstone, 1992; Coombs, 1992), the findings of this study indicate that all the leadership groups expressed concerns about the impact of distance learning on faculty-student interaction.

Organizational and instructional change is achieved by building trust and confidence and is hindered by conflict and apprehension (Bennis and Nanus, 1985). Administrators who see distance education as a means of improving services to their communities will need the support of the chairs who must embrace the use of distance technology. Without the support of all leadership groups, the practice of distance education will remain on the margin of practice in the community college. If, however, all leadership groups believe in the viability of distance education, they will work collaboratively to implement these programs. This study identified some important areas of difference between chairs and other community college leadership groups. In the future, research must address the circumstances that contribute to differences among leadership groups. The involvement of all leadership groups will be necessary if community colleges are to make the transition from conventional approaches to visionary approaches for meeting the changing needs of the communities they serve.

References

Ansari, M. M. Economics of Distance Higher Education. New Delhi: Concept, 1992.

Beaudoin, M. F. "The Instructor's Changing Role in Distance Education." American Journal of Distance Education, 1990, 4 (2), 21–29.

Bennis, W., and Nanus, B. Leaders: The Strategies for Taking Charge. New York: Harper-Collins, 1985.

Brey, R. U.S. Postsecondary Distance Learning Programs in the 1990s: A Decade of Growth. (Report No. JC 920 023). Washington, D.C.: Instructional Telecommunications Consortium, American Association of Community and Junior Colleges, 1991. (ED 340 418)

Bunting, L. D. "First Step in the Feasibility of Interactive Satellite Communication Between the Member Institutions of the League for Innovation in the Community College." Unpublished doctoral dissertation, Northern Arizona University, 1989. Dissertation Abstracts International, 1989, 51 (1), 61A.

Clark, T. "Attitudes of Higher Education Faculty Toward Distance Education: A National Survey." American Journal of Distance Education, 1993, 19–33.

Coombs, N. "Teaching in the Information Age." EDUCOM, Mar./Apr. 1992, pp. 28–31.

Dillon, C. "Faculty Rewards and Instructional Telecommunications: A View from the Telecourse Faculty." American Journal of Distance Education, 1989, 3 (2), 35–43.

Duning, B. S., Van Kekerix, M. J., and Zaborowski, L. M. Reaching Learners Through Telecommunications: Management and Leadership Strategies for Higher Education. San Francisco: Jossey-Bass, 1993.

Gunawardena, C. N. "Integrating Telecommunications Systems to Reach Distance Learners." American Journal of Distance Education, 1990, 4 (3), 38–46.

Hart, P. K. "An Investigation into the Feasibility of Interactive Distance Education Courses at Northwestern Michigan College." Unpublished thesis, Ferris State University, Big Rapids, Mich., 1994.

Kozma, R. "A Grounded Theory of Instructional Innovation in Higher Education." Journal of Higher Education, 1985, 56 (3), 300–319.

Levin, H. M. New Techniques for Evaluation. Thousand Oaks, Calif: Sage, 1981.

Levine, T. Going the Distance: A Handbook for Developing Distance Degree Programs Using Television Courses and Telecommunications Technologies. Bethesda, Md.: T. Levine, 1992.

Mace, J. "Educational Media and Economic Analysis." Media in Education and Development, 1982, 15 (2), 91–93.

Markwood, R. A., and Johnstone, S. M. (eds.). New Pathways to a Degree. Boulder, Colo.: Western Cooperative for Educational Telecommunications, 1992.

Moore, M. G. Contemporary Issues in American Distance Education. New York: Pergamon Press, 1990.

Rumble, G. "Activity Costing in Mixed-Mode Institutions: A Report Based on a Study of Deakin University." Deakin Open Education Monograph No. 2. Victoria, Australia: Deakin University, 1986.

Rumble, G. "The Economics of Mass Distance Education." Prospects, 1988, *18* (1), 91–102.
Tucker, A., and Bryan, R. The Academic Dean: Dove, Dragon or Diplomat. Washington, D.C.: American Council on Education, 1989.
Uveges, J. A. The Dimensions of Public Administration: Introductory Readings. Boston: Holbrook Press, 1971.
Verduin, J. R., and Clark, T. A. Distance Education: The Foundations of Effective Practice. San Francisco: Jossey-Bass, 1991.

DOUGLAS H. LAPE is vice president for administrative services at Northwestern Michigan College. He is also the chief financial officer and responsible for voice, video, and data technology development.

PATRICIA K. HART is controller at Northwestern Michigan College. She was named the 1996 National Outstanding Business Officer by the National Community College Business Officers Association.

This chapter explores the role of the community college in the development of state policies regarding distance learning.

From the Margin to the Mainstream: State-Level Policy and Planning for Distance Education

Patricia Kovel-Jarboe

Until quite recently, most states have had few if any policies that addressed distance education. Institutions offering courses, degrees, and programs at a distance were often in the position of having either to argue about why they should be exempt from particular policies and procedures or to plead to be allowed to take advantage of opportunities that were largely closed to them and their students. To move distance education from the margin to the mainstream of higher education, policy and planning must address the unique needs of distance education providers and learners.

Community colleges will experience significant change as they adapt to the future. Gross (1995) states that the future of the "new" community college will be shaped by three factors—technology, society, and policy. Taylor and Maas (1995) identify more than a dozen characteristics of the community college of the future requiring adjustments in state higher education policy.

For the purpose of analysis and discussion of policy, this chapter adopts a stakeholder perspective. This approach means that one must know who the stakeholders are and understand their assumptions and expectations; it does not assume the dominance or preeminence of any one group or institution. Thus it can accommodate a wide variety of viewpoints (stakes) and interests (Kovel-Jarboe, 1990).

This chapter describes the major factors that emerged from the findings of a study supported by the Fund for the Improvement of Post-Secondary Education and the State Higher Education Executive Officers (FIPSE/SHEEO) in the state of Minnesota. These factors must be addressed by states as they develop policies designed to bring distance education into the mainstream of higher education.

Design of the Study

The FIPSE/SHEEO project was designed to examine possible changes in post-secondary education that would make education more cost-effective and learner-centered. Ultimately the Minnesota Higher Education Coordinating Board became part of this multistate project. Under the sponsorship of SHEEO and with financial support from FIPSE, Minnesota's contribution to the project was an examination of the issues related to distance education.

Approximately two hundred faculty, staff, administrators, and students in Minnesota's public and private postsecondary institutions, including community colleges, were surveyed regarding four possible futures for higher education, ranging from "status quo" to "dramatic change." The subjects were asked in forced-choice questions to indicate how attractive the future appeared to them, their peers, and their campuses.

Using response data, several policy areas were identified as having a significant interaction with distance education (Kovel-Jarboe, 1994). These included quality, student and academic support services, decision-making structures, mission, program and site approval, infrastructure, and financial aid.

Findings

These findings are consistent with other recent analyses. Notably, Hezel (1993) lists thirteen categories of policy requiring attention at the national or state level. Still others have argued the need for state-level policymaking in one or more areas related to the provision of distance education (Gillespie, Jonsen, and Witherspoon, 1987; McGill and Jonsen, 1987; Mugridge, 1996; Schweiger, 1994). In addition, a number of authors confine their policy discussions to technology and telecommunications (Dively, 1987; Gallagher and Hatfield, 1989; Reilly and Gulliver, 1995; Whittington, 1990). Overall, these issues are remarkably similar to the findings of a study conducted over a decade ago that addressed quality in "long distance learning via telecommunications." Sponsored by the Council on Postsecondary Accreditation and SHEEO, Project ALLTEL (Chaloux, 1985) included a series of recommendations that addressed consumer protection, learner outcomes, and various practices related to state authorization of distance learning.

Critical Policy Issues

The balance of this chapter examines the five broad policy clusters identified in the FIPSE/SHEEO study: quality; student support; human and financial resources; governance, mission, and programs; and infrastructure. Most of these policy areas intersect with institutional and state-level responsibilities, while some are significantly affected by what happens in the federal policy-making arena.

Quality Assurance. Quality is a frequently cited concern associated with distance education. The very meaning of a course credit, degree, certificate, or other credential is perceived to be at risk unless appropriate measures are implemented to protect quality. But views of quality vary considerably, as do the approaches states might take in assuring it. Policymakers must be careful to make sure quality does not become a codeword for protectionism either by applying a higher standard to nontraditional delivery systems or by allowing a single body (regulatory agency, governing board, or faculty committee) to control the quality approval process.

Traditional strategies for controlling quality in educational offerings are primarily regulatory. They include registration, certification, and accreditation of programs and institutions. However, quality assurance is shifting from a tradition of regulation to one characterized as loosening or deregulating some or all higher education policies. Some state higher education agencies are considering shifting the emphasis away from oversight of programs and institutions; instead, the state would focus on educating the consumers of higher education. A number of factors are driving consideration of this strategy, including the difficulty of regulating program delivery in a technology-mediated environment, the movement to adopt a definition of quality that is consistent with the tenets of continuous quality improvement, and the lack of resources available to continue monitoring and oversight required in highly regulated systems. Distance education forces us to alter our understanding of the purpose of and audience for education, and policies must reflect that shift. Current quality indicators such as seat time or contact hours and requirements for predetermined outcomes may be meaningless in the distributed learning environment. Discussion of quality assurance must focus upon what is the best measure of student learning and how can we report this to the parties that have traditionally relied on transcripts, certificates, and other credentials.

Distance educators in community colleges should consider whether they or their students are disadvantaged by existing policies that address quality assurance. They already may be particularly attentive to policies that use time-to-degree or credit versus noncredit loads as part of funding formulae, as well as closely examining the way distant learners are counted for formula-funded activities. However, depending on the way in which distance learning opportunities are implemented, these larger and more fundamental issues may be of increasing concern to community colleges.

For instance, community colleges may value the quick response they can make to local community needs, perhaps assisted by learning packages developed elsewhere. They may also be constrained in developing their own course modules by lack of appropriate faculty expertise. Off-the-shelf courseware may also provide an attractive means of addressing rapidly fluctuating enrollments in particular fields. Smaller institutions may be at the greatest disadvantage if the use of purchased courseware is restricted, since they are the least likely to have either the production facilities or technical expertise required to develop multimedia course materials and may be more affected by the factors described earlier.

Quality is clearly one area in which stakeholder assumptions and expectations will present many different perspectives. Conflicts are almost certain to arise in any policy debate even within the same group of stakeholders. An example: one student's measure of quality may be the option to carry community-college-earned credits into a four-year institution's degree program, while another student in the same course may expect a direct link between completing that course and moving into a job. Local industry perspectives of quality may differ substantially from a faculty member's perspective of quality. Perhaps the strongest strategy for addressing policies related to quality assurance is to ascertain each group's assumptions and expectations and involve them in the policy discussions.

Because the advent of distance education is pushing the limits of current policy and practice related to quality assurance, it may appear to some that distance educators and administrators are not concerned with quality and might wish to eliminate all attempts at regulation. If distance education is to move from the margin to the mainstream, distance educators must demonstrate that they are in favor of meaningful measures of quality (that is, learner achievement) that are applicable across teaching modes and learning activities.

Student Support. Student support policies include the entire range of institutional programs and resources that support student learning and personal development. Access to student support services has been shown to be a critical factor in learner success (Tinto, 1993; Voorhees, 1987). Learners must be able to choose among programs and institutions, and select from an array of delivery options and support services. Libraries, financial aid, advising, counseling, mentoring, and opportunities for social interaction with other learners and faculty are some of the support mechanisms important to student learning and development. Although these areas are generally considered the purview of the institution or campus, state policies become increasingly important as telecommunications increases opportunities for access.

Specific state policies may require educational institutions to meet a minimum level of support services. Some institutions may find contracting for certain distance learning services to be a cost-effective and high-quality alternative to administering the service using campus resources. For example, a community college that offers courses via computer (perhaps through a Web server) may arrange with a commercial computer center or even a computer retailer to provide "help desk" support for students who experience technical difficulties in configuring and using their equipment for course access. Also, state policies can encourage interinstitutional collaboration to maximize access. For instance, requiring a statewide library card—a card that provides access to all college library services for all students—or establishing minimum standards for receiving sites or learning centers are two examples of state-level responsibility. If an institution wishes to present its students with twenty-four-hour-a-day, seven-day-a-week access to instruction, some may feel it is reasonable to expect that students will have the same hours of access to support services. Others may determine that more limited hours of service are appropriate. As protectors of consumer interests, state higher education agencies may become involved in these decisions.

Financial aid and other federal or state programs will require modification if they are to serve the needs of lifelong learners, many of whom will take advantage of the availability and convenience of off-campus programs. Some of the concerns associated with financial aid for distant learners have already engendered considerable discussion. Should so-called full-time students who take courses from multiple institutions during a single time period be eligible for aid? What about students who receive modular instruction, such as single units of instruction offered as remediation rather than courses? Do some of the emerging technology-based methods of delivering instruction to remote learners re-create a traditional classroom, thus gaining certain advantages for financial aid seekers? Or are they more like correspondence study, thus, in most cases, making financial aid far more problematic?

Other stakeholders with concerns in the area of financial aid could include local lending institutions and state banking authorities. Community college staff (librarians, advisers, and so on) form another group with definite interests in any policy changes related to academic and support services. The diversity of the community college student population will also bring a diversity of learning styles, motivation, and technological competence. Community colleges may also have high percentages of part-time learners—already at a disadvantage in securing financial aid and access to technology. For these reasons, community colleges must begin to marshal the data available on their students' particular needs and quickly introduce them in policy debates.

Human and Financial Resources. Even the most cursory review of the literature on institutional change suggests that little if any benefit will be derived from the tremendous potential associated with distance education without considerable attention to human development. Faculty must be able to choose to use and adapt instructional technology and institutions must be able to choose when and how to implement distance education. Human and financial resources may appear to be primarily internal to the institution, yet collective bargaining agreements, faculty productivity, and resource allocation are examples of issues in which state policies may come into play.

Important policy considerations include how to compensate faculty for distance teaching, whether through incentive pay or reduced course loads. In addition, the terms under which courseware may be developed, marketed outside the institution, or used after the developer ceases to be employed by the institution are also important issues. Questions such as how many students can and should be accommodated in a single course offering are of vital interest to faculty.

Sometimes these policies will give less emphasis to regulating or restricting activities and more attention to allowing or encouraging certain activities.

Faculty accustomed to the relative security of the classroom may find the increased visibility of telecommunications teaching a source of anxiety. Likewise the shift from the autonomy of traditional teaching to team approaches to learning may cause faculty to struggle with their roles and relationships with nonprofessional and even nonacademic support personnel. Distance learning requires that faculty adopt new roles and responsibilities. Policies that address faculty development will help make the transition to the new learning environment an opportunity for faculty rather than a threat.

From the foregoing it is easy to see why faculty governance bodies such as faculty senates and collective bargaining organizations are beginning to express concerns about the impact distance education policies will have on the conditions of faculty employment. When distance learning is a marginal aspect of campus life, it is tempting to offer incentives (often monetary) to entice faculty to design and deliver distance education offerings. In many cases this can be done without implementing new policy. As distance learning comes to represent the mainstream of instructional practice, the incentive structure may change (or disappear), and new policies will almost certainly be required.

Important financial issues to be addressed include what distant learners should pay—a convenience or equipment surcharge or a differential tuition (either higher or lower than on-campus students), or a fee for services and activities available to on-campus students—and how these revenues are to be distributed.

When multiple institutions are involved in jointly providing a distance education program, state policy may deal with the question of who earns credit for the headcount, a particular concern in jurisdictions in which headcount accounts for a sizable portion of state-level funding (Toby Levine Communications, 1992).

Governance, Mission, and Programs. Geographic service areas have been implicit in much of the policy relating to institutional mission. Policies have often been more about differentiating among types of institutions in a specific locale and less about duplication of programs in various parts of the state. As it has become feasible to deliver courses, programs, and whole degrees without regard to the location of the learner, mission may be acquiring a new meaning. Notions of duplication, overlap, and uniqueness shift dramatically with permeable geographic boundaries.

With both traditional and emerging institutions providing virtual instruction, and with credit banks poised to offer degrees, states begin to face the question of what constitutes a postsecondary institution. For example, should at least some of the education provided in the workplace under the auspices of the employing organization be usable toward a degree or credential?

Just as regulatory bodies and legislatures developed reciprocity agreements to expand educational choice and access in their jurisdictions, they will have to deal with the opportunities and challenges created by the transparency of state (and national) boundaries to distance education. Some state policies, such as those relating to service areas, may be abandoned in favor of a tighter rein on marketing, advertising, and recruitment. Other states may deal explicitly with the issue of competition by developing mechanisms to referee disputes and conflicts. Still other states will focus their efforts on ensuring that distance education programs have a reasonable expectation of continuity (that students who matriculate will be able to complete the program) and that state-provided resources are used efficiently and, perhaps, equitably. In other words, the concern will be with fiscal accountability.

Another way in which states have responded to the growth of distance education programs and courses is to develop new policies governing transfer of credit. Some states have implemented so-called transfer curricula to facilitate the adoption of two-plus-two agreements between community colleges and four-year institutions. The particular policy issues that arise depend on the model of distance education that a state or institution has adopted. One state might choose an approach that makes it easy for students to collect and transfer credits from multiple institutions back to a home campus. Another state may decide that the best way to serve student needs is to cross-list courses at multiple institutions, so students do not need to transfer credits. Under the second model, does the instructor become a de facto employee of each institution listing the course? Or, might the faculty member remain affiliated with a single institution but be selected and evaluated with the participation of faculty (and students) from all campuses listing the course?

Policies may involve state-level agreement about the broad transferability of a core of courses, common course numbering schemes, and restrictions on which institutions may offer particular (usually introductory) courses. Such policies may apply only to courses offered at a distance (the situation in Oregon as related by Toby Levine Communications) or to those offered comprehensively. State policy may also take the form of simplifying the processes and requirements that individual institutions use to manage the transfer of credit. As noted earlier, some institutions may address related issues through the development of partnerships such as two-plus-two programs.

Infrastructure. Important policy considerations include facilities (studios, classrooms, other sites); technologies (hardware, networks, and software other than courseware); and funding strategies. While finance (discussed in an earlier section) generally has to do with institutional income streams, funding strategy centers on identifying and allocating specific monetary resources to the acquisition, maintenance, and replacement of equipment and facilities that are not used exclusively by a single student or course.

Higher education has yet to find the best formula for funding the development of distance education and instructional technology. Good policy could help establish the right mix of direct public investment, institutional reallocation, and learner fees to support the development, expansion, and maintenance of learning technologies, including the networks that support distance learning. Concomitantly, policy must also address the related issues that arise—telecommunications pricing and the cost to access the information infrastructure. The state policy role may be less important than federal regulation but it is nonetheless influential. State-level education policy that identifies specific services (such as ISDN or ATM) as preferred for the delivery of distance education can, according to Gallagher and Hatfield (1989), create buying power and thus more favorable terms and conditions for that state's purchasers. Another important issue for states is how public utility commissions will address definitions of universal service, rate of return, and regulation that might support distance learning.

Traditional institutions, as well as institutions that target distant learners exclusively, deliver courses, programs, and degrees to students through a broad array of technologies and partnerships. The processes formerly used to approve learning sites will have to change dramatically if they are to continue to provide oversight for instruction that may move directly from the campus (or other originating site) to the learner at home or in the workplace. Rather than focusing primarily on location, approval processes may shift to address curricular coherence and to seek evidence that instructional strategies are appropriate to both content and delivery mechanisms.

The need for learning sites will likely continue. These may be today's campuses retrofitted for independent learners and learning activities, or they may be learning sites located in community centers, places of employment, or other accessible facilities near concentrations of learners. Such centers may be of particular interest to community colleges working with significant numbers of low-income students or the unemployed, who are unlikely to have access through home or workplace to the many kinds of technologies that are used to deliver distance learning opportunities.

Distance learning networks created or acquired with state investment, whether managed within a higher education agency or separately established, are often governed by their own policies. Community colleges should expect to be actively involved in the development of network policies whenever they are participants in those networks. Network policies typically address questions of who has access, what are the program and scheduling priorities, whether or not usage or membership fees will be used to fund equipment replacement costs, and what network-associated costs are a local (campus) responsibility.

Conclusion

Most states are now engaged in or will soon be entering a period of highly active policymaking around issues and opportunities associated with distance education. The current level of activity can be attributed to the increasing importance of distance teaching and learning to the achievement of institutional missions, coupled with the lack of applicable existing policies. Community colleges, especially if they are newcomers to distance education, may wonder if their involvement in policymaking is the best use of limited resources. Also, if institutional representatives to state-level policymaking bodies are not well informed about their campus's efforts in distance education, they may not immediately understand the importance of these discussions to the future of their institutions.

There are compelling reasons for community colleges to be leading players in the state-level policymaking arena. The interaction of campus (institutional) policy and state-level policy is a dynamic process. No institution can do a worthy job of campus planning without an understanding of the governing state (and federal) policies. But, the reverse is also true; that is, state-level policy is better when informed by campus practice and policy. If community colleges are not represented in the process of policymaking, or if they are only weakly represented, state policies as well as campus practices will be the poorer for it.

How then might a community college prepare to participate in state-level policymaking? One possibility is to plan for policymaking simultaneous to the planning for distance education in general. As the shape of a distance education program begins to emerge, key stakeholders should be identified and their needs and expectations articulated. These can then be related to the broad policy categories discussed here. With planning complete, the community college is prepared to implement effective strategies for accomplishing its policy-related goals. Such an approach to distance learning policy may be necessary to ensure the competitiveness of community colleges as educational providers for the future.

References

Chaloux, B. *The Project on Assessing Long Distance Learning Via Telecommunications: Project ALLTEL.* Denver, Colo.: Council on Postsecondary Accreditation and State Higher Education Executive Officers Association, 1985.

Dively, D. "Principles and Guidelines for a Coordinated Telecommunications Plan." In M. McGill and R. Jonsen (eds.), *State Higher Education Policies in the Information Age.* Boulder, Colo.: Western Interstate Commission for Higher Education, 1987.

Gallagher, L., and Hatfield, D. *Distance Learning: Opportunities in Telecommunications Policy and Technology.* Washington, D.C.: Annenberg Washington Program, 1989.

Gillespie, R., Jonsen, R., and Witherspoon, J. "State Higher Education Policies in the Information Age: An Introduction to the Issues." In M. McGill and R. Jonsen (eds.), *State Higher Education Policies in the Information Age.* Boulder, Colo.: Western Interstate Commission for Higher Education, 1987.

Gross, R. "New Mandate for Distance Learning in the Twenty-First Century." *Community College Journal,* 1995, 66 (2), 28–33.

Hezel, R. "National and State Policy Issues in Distance Education: The Issues and Research." In *Distance Education Symposium: Selected Papers, Vol. 2.* University Park, Pa.: American Center for the Study of Distance Education, 1993.

Kovel-Jarboe, P. "Organization and Administration of Distance Education." In M. Moore (ed.), *Contemporary Issues in American Distance Education.* New York: Pergamon Press, 1990, 22–29.

Kovel-Jarboe, P. *Enhancing and Extending Education: The Role of Distance Education in Minnesota.* St. Paul. Minnesota Higher Education Coordinating Board, 1994.

McGill, M., and Jonsen, R. *State Higher Education Policies in the Information Age.* Boulder, Colo.: Western Interstate Commission for Higher Education, 1987.

Mugridge, I. "Remote Delivery of Programs." *DEOSNEWS: The Electronic Journal on Distance*

Education, 1996, 6 (2). [To subscribe, contact ACSDE@PSUVM.PSU.EDU or post the following command to LISTSERV@PSUVM.PSU.EDU: "Subscribe DEOSNEWS," skip one space, then type your first and last name.]

Reilly, K., and Gulliver, K. "Interstate Authorization of Distance Higher Education Via Telecommunications: The Developing National Consensus in Policy and Practice." In M. G. Moore and M. A. Koble (eds.), *Video-Based Telecommunications in Distance Education* (Readings in Distance Education 4). University Park, Pa.: American Center for the Study of Distance Education, 1995.

Schweiger, H. *Open and Distance Learning: Alternative Approaches to the Delivery of Post-Secondary Education.* St. Paul, Minn.: Minnesota Higher Education Coordinating Board, 1994.

Taylor, L., and Maas, M. *Community College of the Future.* Riverside, Calif.: Maas, Rao, Taylor, and Associates, 1995. (ED 381 191)

Tinto, V. *Leaving College: Rethinking the Causes and Cures of Student Attrition.* Chicago: University of Chicago Press, 1993.

Toby Levine Communications, Inc. *Going the Distance: A Handbook for Developing Distance Degree Programs.* Washington, D.C.: Annenberg/CPB Project and PBS Adult Learning Service, 1992.

Voorhees, R. "Toward Building Models of Community College Persistence: A Logit Analysis." *Research in Higher Education,* 1987, 26 (2), 115–129.

Whittington, N. "Characteristics of Good State Instructional Telecommunications Policy for Higher Education: Some Research Considerations." In M. G. Moore (ed.), *Contemporary Issues in American Distance Education.* New York: Pergamon Press, 1990.

PATRICIA KOVEL-JARBOE *has worked in distance learning since 1981 and has a long-standing interest in the roles that institutional and public policies play in the creation of distance learning opportunities. She now consults on distance learning policy-making and is an adjunct faculty member at the University of Minnesota.*

Using technology to develop new collaboration models can help in addressing the complex challenges of delivering comprehensive postsecondary programs in rural communities.

Seamless Education Through Distance Learning: State Policy Initiatives for Community College/ K–12 Partnerships

Suzanna Spears, Randy L. Tatroe

Seamless education implies an educational system in which students can learn through multiple organizational frameworks. This means providing educational opportunities at home, in schools, or in the workplace in a system that integrates training, credit offerings, and mandatory education.

The concept of a seamless educational system linked by distance learning technology is particularly important to rural areas. In the tradition of the land-grant movement, distance education has served to extend learning opportunities to rural areas that lack the educational and information resources of colleges in urban settings. Even though new technologies can provide instant and immediate access to a full range of educational resources, rural communities fear that their needs will not be met as a result of inadequate incentives to develop telecommunications infrastructure in low-population areas (Rural Clearinghouse, 1994).

Given the changing needs of the learner and the growing number of rural residents demanding educational opportunities, partnerships between K–12 schools and community colleges are an important starting place in the exploration of the technological, political, and organizational factors needed to support a seamless education system. Such a system can best assure that students in both secondary and postsecondary institutions can access the education they need, providing a pathway for true lifelong learning.

Following a description of some successful partnerships, this chapter describes how Pikes Peak Community College (PPCC) extended educational opportunities to high school students in rural Colorado.

Exemplary Partnerships

Partnerships must be a part of the plan if we are to realize the potential of distance education as a vehicle for seamless education. However, the key to success requires new approaches to the organizational and policy issues that in the past have served as barriers to integration of services.

In Connecticut, a distance learning partnership involved three local high schools and a cable company, with the purpose of delivering foreign language courses to students. The participants were from an urban high school, an affluent suburban high school. and a high school in a small working-class town. This project was unique in that it demonstrated that telecommunications can be successful in bringing together students from diverse cultures and backgrounds (Pitkoff and Roosen, 1994).

In Texas, a partnership between Southwest Texas State University, San Marcos School District, and San Marcos Telephone Company was formed to help high school students improve their mathematics skills via a curriculum delivered by a fiber-optic network (Chavkin, Feyl, Kennedy, and Carter, 1994). The underlying premise was that schools cannot solve educational problems by themselves, and that families, schools, businesses, and communities must work together. Tutoring, offered both on site and through the interactive network, and a Homework Hotline were also part of the system. Unique to this partnership, and illustrative of the potential role of community services, was the participation of social workers who counseled and provided services to family members, teachers, and community agencies. Some participants believed this type of support was a contributing factor to student success.

The New Mexico Eastern Plains Interactive TV Cooperative was created in 1990, initiated by the local telephone company. This system allowed rural high schools to share curricula, provided college courses through a rural community college, and offered medical training and technical support with the participation of the Texas Tech Health Sciences Center in Lubbock (Sullivan, Jolly, Foster, and Tompkins, 1993).

In 1991, the State University of New York (SUNY), in concert with the U.S. Department of Education, several K–12 school districts, and two cable TV systems, developed a program to deliver interactive multimedia curricula to learners at home. Mathematics was given the highest priority. Two special elements of this project were that students took computer equipment home, and that participating teachers attended a five-day institute to prepare them to teach on TV. The program was sponsored by such diverse organizations as the New York State Theater Institute and the television production staff at SUNY. It was so successful that SUNY is now collaborating with other businesses and local school districts and the Board of Cooperative Educational Services to deliver similar programs (Benson, 1994).

The Pikes Peak Case Study

Pikes Peak Community College serves four counties in east-central Colorado covering 4,539 square miles with a population of approximately 475,000. Most of the service area is rural ranch land but approximately one-fifth is in the Front Range of the Rocky Mountains. The population is concentrated in the metropolitan area of Colorado Springs, but small towns dot the plains to the east and the mountains to the west. Distance, lack of transportation, and unpredictable weather add to the difficulties rural citizens encounter when seeking high school courses and postsecondary education. PPCC has struggled for years with the problem of providing educational services to the communities on the plains and in the mountains. Although the college was committed to its mission of serving all communities, attempts to deliver on-site courses to these sparsely populated areas frequently resulted in low enrollment or lack of access to qualified faculty, and subsequent course cancellations. Technology offered Pikes Peak a solution.

Technological Infrastructure:
The Power of Delivery Systems

The following delivery options are in use by PPCC and by one or more of its partners.

Interactive Television. The Instructional Television Fixed Station (ITFS) delivers live, interactive courses for college and high school students. Interactivity is achieved through an audio bridge that connects distant learners at all classroom sites with the instructor during the class period. Students at home must call in on an 800 number to communicate with the instructor during the class period.

Telecourses. Courses by nationally known telecourse producers are delivered to the distant learner through local PBS stations or by the college's ITFS station.

Internet. Courses using the Internet have been available since fall 1995. Depending on the course structure, students interact with the instructor through an e-mail address, and in some cases, communicate on-line in real time through servers located at the college.

Print-Based Independent Study. For students who need maximum flexibility for course completion, several independent study courses were developed. Student packets include a course syllabus with expected student outcomes; instructions for course completion, testing, and contact with faculty; textbooks, workbooks, and other research and supplemental materials.

Audio-Graphics. Computer-generated graphics were delivered over regular telephone lines. Students interacted with the instructor and other students through an audio bridge. Courses were developed with a grant from the Colorado Department of Education.

On-Site Delivery. When a group of ten qualified individuals was available at a site, the college provided a faculty member to teach a course at that location.

Driving the Partnership:
The Needs of the Lifelong Learner

Current career development models in both the K–12 and the postsecondary environments identify the individual as a lifelong learner. The skills and competencies we use today may no longer serve in tomorrow's workplace, so an educational system is needed that allows us to gain necessary skills and competencies regardless of location. This model allows students of various ages, education and experience backgrounds, and geographic locations to access the education and training needed to continue to be active citizens.

State Policy Forces. During the late 1980s, the Colorado Department of Education recommended that K–12 school districts look at articulation agreements with local community colleges to provide programs that could offer both general and technical education. Funds were running short in state coffers and new legislation had significantly changed the way school districts would receive funding. Articulation agreements were negotiated between individual school districts and their local colleges to provide a pathway for students to move between these two entities, carrying credits from high school to college, or completing some college credits before graduating from high school. The primary purpose was to share resources such as faculty among school districts and colleges, and to offer a broad-based curriculum in all regions of the state.

While these issues were being addressed at the local level, the state legislature, the Colorado Commission for Higher Education, and statewide committees of the Colorado Community College and Occupational Education System were also putting together policies and initiatives that would encourage the growth of partnerships between K–12 and postsecondary institutions.

Colorado Post-Secondary Options Act. This piece of legislation required school districts to fund the costs of qualified high school students to take college courses on local college campuses, at college outreach centers, or through college programs offered at the high schools. The bill also required school districts and colleges to negotiate a reasonable cost for students to attend these courses. The courses were to be offered for both high school and college credit so that a student could take advantage of a broader curriculum than the high school might have been able to offer, and also allow the student to get a jump on college coursework. Another important facet of this program was that both the school districts and the community colleges were encouraged to allow qualified community members to enroll in the college courses that were offered at the high schools.

Colorado CORE Curriculum Agreement. Several forces worked together from 1986 to 1988 to develop a core curriculum of general education courses to be offered by the community colleges. This curriculum was designed to transfer to almost all of the state's four-year institutions to fulfill lower-division general education requirements. The core currently contains fifty-four courses and is reviewed annually by faculty representatives from the community colleges and four-year institutions. This policy provided a level of security for students who moved from community to community within the state, since they would be able to take their credits with them and continue with the same curriculum at their new schools.

Award of Credit for Standardized Exam. In 1987, the Colorado Community College and Occupational Education System convened a task force with representatives from each of the eleven state system community colleges to investigate the feasibility of a policy on credit for prior learning. In 1989, a permanent policy was approved after a one-year trial run. This policy established a system at all state community colleges that allowed adults with various backgrounds to have their experiences evaluated. If there was documented evidence of college-level learning, credit was to be awarded to the student. One method of evaluation was the use of standardized tests to include the CLEP, DANTES, and ACT/PEP. After implementation of the policy, it became evident that colleges were awarding different credits for the same tests. There was even use of differing scores for the award of credit. The Prior Learning Task Force took up the challenge of standardizing the courses, credits, and scores to be used in awarding credit.

State Reimbursement Procedures for Student Enrollment. A recent change to the reporting guidelines for Colorado's colleges and universities now allows for more flexibility with distance education enrollments in determining eligibility for state reimbursement dollars. If there is regular interaction between students and faculty, colleges can count enrollments, even if they should occur outside of an officially defined service area (as long as they are within the state). This expanded procedure provides an opportunity for school districts and colleges to work together to offer programs that benefit the students, faculty, and the local communities.

Regional Initiatives. Beyond the local community and the state level, three regional initiatives have emerged that have already influenced, or will influence the continued growth of this model.

Western Interstate Commission for Higher Education (WICHE). In 1995, WICHE developed a set of principles to assess quality in distance education. By using these *Principles of Good Practice for Distance Education Programs,* a partnership can be sure that all areas of student and faculty support are included in a program plan. In addition, the implementation of the principles better assures that the distance education program provides a quality learning experience.

Western Governors University. In February 1996, the Western Governors Association developed a concept of a multifaceted partnership providing yet another face to the seamless education system. Chapter Seven describes this partnership in more detail.

Going the Distance Project. In 1992, the Public Broadcasting System (PBS) realized that larger numbers of adults were taking advantage of college courses through partnerships between local PBS affiliates and postsecondary institutions in the areas they served. Over the next year, PBS worked with a group of experts representing higher education, telecourse producers, and telecommunications organizations to determine the feasibility of creating a two-year transfer degree program offered via public broadcasting. Pilot programming was announced in 1994, promising a new dimension of partnerships in seamless education.

The Development of the Partnership

The PPCC was approached by a private wireless cable company, American Telecasting, Inc. (ATI), interested in developing a partnership for the use of an Instructional Television Fixed Station (ITFS). ATI saw the provision of educational services as an important strategy for increasing its subscriber base. ATI provided the installation of the equipment at PPCC and eighteen school sites, technical support, and free access to the network.

Simultaneously, a consortium of school districts in the Pikes Peak region had received a grant from the Colorado Department of Education to develop and implement a series of courses over an educational network incorporating audio-graphic equipment. The school districts that were tied into the audio-graphic network invited PPCC to join them; their hope was that PPCC would deliver college courses over the system to complement the current high school offerings. PPCC began meeting with district representatives, acting as a liaison between the districts and the other community colleges that were offering courses over this system. This provided the district with the program access they were looking for.

In a further expansion of partnerships with K–12 educators, PPCC analyzed the vocational training it was offering to limited numbers of students in eighteen different school districts. The Area Vocational Program (AVP) primarily provided these services by busing students to the Colorado Springs campus. Some students were traveling as much as an hour and a half each way. The AVP provided another network for the College to use to assess the needs of schools and local communities. Representatives from most of the AVP school districts also sat on the Pikes Peak Region Consortium.

These three events became the foundation of the partnership that would eventually include eighteen school districts, a community college, representation from local businesses providing telecommunications services, and universities interested in participating in a seamless education system.

The model now offered high school curricula delivered from PPCC to the schools and into homes (over the wireless cable company's system) in urban and rural communities. These courses enabled districts to share in the cost of course delivery and expand their own offerings, even if they only had a few students interested in the content area. In addition, college courses were delivered over the system, providing access for high school students and adults from the community, regardless of the number of interested individuals. Since courses were delivered from the college's main campus, full-and part-time faculty were readily available to provide instruction. As more adults became interested in the program, the concept of credit for prior learning was included to allow the use of standardized tests for the completion of some of the degree requirements. Rural residents can now plan a program of lifelong learning that fits their needs and interests, as four-year institutions add access to upper-level and graduate coursework.

Currently in development is a program that will allow high school students to complete a two-year degree program at a distance, by taking college-level courses through a variety of delivery modalities during their traditional senior year and a fifth year. At the end of the fifth year, they will be awarded a two-year associate of arts degree from PPCC and a high school diploma from their home institution.

Another enhancement of the model has occurred with the inclusion of multiple delivery systems. Coursework can be completed through live, on-site courses (if enrollment is sufficient) sometimes taught by local high school faculty approved by the community college. The work can also be completed through the one-way video and two-way audio system, through traditional telecourses offered over the local PBS network, and through computer courses accessible through the Internet.

Seamless education has offered a model of success for all partners. High schools, through support of the ATI partnership, receive college courses delivered in a different medium. ATI, by providing antennas and control boxes to the school districts, increases viewership in rural areas. In addition, colleges are attracting new students, and the statewide credit for prior learning program encourages adults in different communities to explore credit award possibilities. Setting up telecommunications classrooms in rural high schools could result in adults making use of these facilities in the evening or on weekends.

Development of Interinstitutional Policy and Procedures

Once the process started, it was important to formalize communication among the partners—administrators, superintendents, and principals, as well as technical staff from the districts. Subcommittees were formed to work out details, monitor progress toward goals, and make reports to a larger group. Rather than attempting to begin with a complete degree program, the partnership began by offering individual courses, giving faculty the opportunity to experience distance learning on a small scale before making a wholesale commitment. But it soon became apparent that there were advantages in designing a continuous program of lifelong learning.

Class Size Issues. Policies were formulated to serve students who had completed high school. If there was a group of at least ten students, PPCC could send a faculty member to teach the course, on site. If there were fewer than ten, a distant delivery mode would be used. Other challenges were identified such as a common hour and common days available. Also, the PPCC asked the school districts to consider allowing parents and other community adults to attend either the live on-site courses or the telecommunicated ones. Finally, the groups looked at the possible addition of the credit for prior learning component for adults. It was apparent that PPCC needed to develop a degree plan incorporating all the various options so that a potential user could define and progress through a total education.

Marketing. The school districts immediately started advertising among their student bodies the availability of new foreign language classes, and enrollment surged. School districts used parent meetings and other open-school activities to talk about the opportunities. Class schedules were sent home in newsletters. PPCC included information on the expanded distance learning courses in its term class schedules, and adults began to enroll. The college's Division of Extended Studies put together an external degree plan brochure, identifying the process for credit awards and subsequent enrollment in distant learning courses. In addition, the PPCC Telecommunications Division student handbook includes information on planning a degree using the new resources.

Special target populations were also identified that could benefit from distance education programs, and these groups were invited to attend information sessions.

Technical and Student Support. Initially, ATI was called to provide service in the event of a malfunction of broadcast equipment. On occasion there was an atmospheric reason for a loss of signal, but most often such problems occurred because of a technical mistake at either the sending site or the receiving site. PPCC now provides training to technicians at all sites.

Other needed services included placement testing, program advising, financial aid application assistance, textbook delivery, access to support materials and faculty, and examination proctoring. Program evaluation became a critical component in evaluating student frustrations and successes with the new programs. Many of these services are now made available on-line or via fax for the distant student.

Scheduling. To address the vagaries of schedules at different schools, a single schedule is prepared that accommodates the majority of the schools, while the remaining schools are required to alter their daily or weekly schedules or tape the classes for viewing at a later time. Schools that tape the programs cannot take full advantage of the interactivity and direct connection with the instructor. In one unique situation, students were bused, on a week-by-week basis, between two rural high schools.

Preliminary Evaluation of Student Progress

From spring 1993 to spring 1996, there were 1,956 distant learner enrollments at PPCC. Of those enrollments, 40 were high school students participating at a distance in college-level courses. Twenty of those students received passing grades while the remainder received unsatisfactory grades or withdrew. Comparing the adult learners during the same period, 1,320 (68.9 percent) received passing grades, while 596 (31.1 percent) received unsatisfactory grades or withdrew.

Upon investigation of the noncompleters, the source of difficulty appears to be inadequate preenrollment counseling. High school students, for example, enrolled in the distance learning courses without the benefit of testing to evaluate their chances of success.

A statewide study by the Telecommunications Cooperative for Colorado's Colleges (TELECOOP) indicated that one-way video and two-way audio systems had a greater number of noncompleters. The study compared the completion rates of students enrolled in a variety of telecommunications systems currently in use in Colorado for the 1995–96 academic year (TELECOOP Annual Report, 1996).

This information has led PPCC and the high schools to work more closely together to structure the out-of-class learning activities for high school students. High school counselors have also begun to screen students more closely in preparation for participating in college-level courses.

The technology and faculty resources are continually being challenged by the distant learner. Course offerings using interactive television have almost doubled in the first two years of operation and are expected to continue to grow. The numbers of courses offered using Internet access are also attracting increasing numbers of students.

Conclusion

State and regional initiatives coupled with interest from a private telecommunications provider proved crucial to the development of a unique educational collaboration. At the regional level, the WICHE guidelines established minimum quality standards for the distance learning partnership. In addition, the example of the new Western Governors University provided a concept for model building. Finally, the Going the Distance Project provided an additional outlet for program offerings.

At the state level, the Colorado Post-Secondary Options Act and the State Reimbursement Procedures for Student Enrollment policy provide financial incentives for this partnership—the former by providing a funding source through encouraging school districts to share the cost burden, and the latter by providing state support for distant learners. State polices also expanded academic opportunities by supporting articulation and experiential learning. The

Colorado CORE Curriculum Agreement provided for increased transferability of college courses. Adult participation was encouraged by the Award of Credit or Standardized Exams policy. These policies helped create a climate of collaboration among the partners and fostered the development of a market for telecommunications providers. In addition, the establishment of a formal inter-institutional mechanism of communication supported the development policies and procedures that encouraged participation and quality improvement.

Several factors remain crucial and offer opportunity for broader participation by community colleges in collaborative distance learning ventures: increased scrutiny and debate about how tax dollars are spent on education; the dynamic economic environment, which requires that individuals learn new skills or acquire additional information; and the rapidly increasing population in areas that cannot acquire structures fast enough to satisfy demand. These issues place even greater pressure on rural K–12 school districts and other agencies to develop collaborative programs that result in enhanced curricula for their students and professional development activities for their faculty. The community college should be at the heart of these collaborative models.

References

Benson, G. *SUNY/K–12 Learning Technology Partnerships for Enhancing Educational Opportunities in Schools and Homes,* Albany, N.Y.: Office of Educational Technology, State University of New York, 1994. (ED 375 808)

Chavkin, N., Feyl, N., Kennedy, P., and Carter, M. "Distance Learning Partnerships for Underserved Learners." *TechTrends,* 1994, *39* (5), 30, 37–38.

Pitkoff, E., and Roosen, E. "New Technology, New Attitudes Provide Language Instruction." *NAASP Bulletin,* 1994, *78* (563), 37–41.

Rural Clearinghouse for Lifelong Education and Development. "Distance Learning Technologies Link Adults to Educational Programming Opportunities." *Rural Clearinghouse Digest,* 1994, *1* (2), 3–8.

Sullivan, M., Jolly, D., Foster, D., and Tompkins, R. "Rural Communities Communicating: The Emergence of Two-Way Interactive Video in Southwestern, Rural, Small Schools, 1993." Paper presented at the annual meeting of the National Rural Education Association, Burlington, Vt., Oct. 12–18, 1993. (ED 367 512)

TELECOOP Annual Report. Littleton, Colo.: Telecommunications Cooperative for Colorado's Colleges, 1996.

Western Interstate Commission for Higher Education. *When Distance Education Crosses State Boundaries: Western States Policies 1995.* Boulder, Colo.: Western Interstate Commission for Higher Education, 1995.

SUZANNA SPEARS is dean for arts, sciences, and instructional development at Morgan Community College. The college's service area is over 11,000 square miles, and is exclusively made up of rural communities.

RANDY L. TATROE is interim director of the Telecommunications Division at Pikes Peak Community College. Although the institution sits in an urban setting, the bulk of its geographic service area is rural.

This case study describes how one state views technology as a solution to meeting increased demand for higher education from an increasingly diverse student population with a declining proportion of state revenues.

Reducing Time-to-Degree with Distance Learning: Are We Closer Now Than When We Started?

Patrick Dallet, John H. Opper

The onset of the 1990s found Florida faced with the prospect of burgeoning demand for access to postsecondary education coupled with increased needs for health and social services, law enforcement, and corrections. This is not a unique situation among the states, but given Florida's diverse population and rapid growth, it is a particularly daunting one. While access at point-of-entry to college is an important issue in Florida, access to the degree is equally critical. Ensuring that enrolled students have the opportunity to succeed in their quest for a degree in an efficient and effective manner requires initiatives beyond those aimed at point-of-entry. For example, the goal of reducing time-to-degree resulted in a number of initiatives at both the state and institutional levels, including a recommitment to articulation between two- and four-year institutions, enhanced student advising, caps on the number of credits required for a degree, student degree contracts, and incentives and penalties related to excess student hours.

Against this background, distance learning and the use of telecommunications to deliver instruction have been the subject of intense debate, study, and legislation as policymakers, administrators, faculty, and students have seized upon the potential of these tools to solve the access and resource challenges. The decision we face in Florida is whether distance education can help us make more effective use of resources to broaden access, address diverse needs, and reduce time-to-degree.

Scope of the Problem

Since the early 1980s, Florida's public postsecondary institutions have received a steadily declining share of state general revenue, from 15 percent in 1987–88 to 12 percent in 1996–97. In contrast, the percentage of general revenue support for corrections and juvenile justice has more than doubled (from 6 percent to over 9 percent) during the same period (Office of Planning and Budgeting, 1996). This restricted situation is compounded by tuition rates that rank near the bottom among the states (university tuition for state residents is forty-ninth in the nation) and dramatic projected growth in demand (Washington State Higher Education Coordinating Board, 1997). Over the next ten years, the number of public high school graduates will increase about 42 percent, to some 135,000 (Miller, 1996). Faced with a serious shortage of capital construction funds as well, Florida is pursuing alternative strategies to improve the efficiency of the current delivery system rather than greatly expand physical capacity.

The 1995 Florida Legislature enacted comprehensive legislation designed to improve the progress of students. The legislation provided for the reduction and standardization in the number of hours required for a degree (with the Associate of Arts degree and Bachelors of Arts or Sciences limited to 60 and 120 semester hours respectively). It also called for the development of common prerequisites for each program of study to aid in the articulation process, an improved student advising system, and the increased involvement of private higher education in alleviating demand in selected access programs (Laws of Florida, 1995). Also during the 1995 legislative session, distance learning was addressed as part of the telecommunications reauthorization. The Florida Distance Learning Network was established as a coordinating oversight body to support the use of technology and distance learning in enhancing student access and success as a result of the 1996 Education Facilities Infrastructure Improvement Act. This group—made up of representatives of government, business, and education—has been meeting for more than a year, inventorying existing resources and identifying distance learning needs and strategies to address them.

Bottleneck Courses

The Florida Postsecondary Education Planning Commission received grant support from the State Higher Education Officers and the Fund for the Improvement of Postsecondary Education as part of a national 1995–96 "Redesigning Higher Education" project. Subsequently named Improving Access Through Technology (IATT), this project investigated the factors associated with lengthened time-to-degree. Interviews were conducted with provosts, academic vice presidents, undergraduate deans, registrars, and faculty members to explore the commonly identified causes of course bottlenecks (scheduling, faculty productivity, limited faculty lines, enrollment growth).

After further analysis of student course enrollment data, the commission targeted core undergraduate courses with low completion rates—bottlenecks—as an area of focus. With the help of a statewide steering committee, high-enrollment courses with high failure or withdrawal rates were selected for further attention.

Scanning the Systems

A review of data from all community colleges and a sample of state universities indicated, perhaps not surprisingly, that the majority of such bottleneck courses were in mathematics and science. In the community colleges, the figures were particularly dramatic in some cases. In 1994, only 47 percent of 18,377 community college students enrolled in intermediate algebra successfully completed this course. High-demand courses were defined as courses with at least 840 enrollments. Of the 115 high-enrollment courses identified, 9 were in English and 14 in mathematics and statistics. The analysis of community college withdrawal and failure rates indicated that 38 percent of all enrollments in high-demand courses could be accounted for in English and mathematics. In addition, over 40 percent of needed retakes are the result of these same courses, which represent only 5 percent of the total systemwide offerings. One of the most interesting findings from the site visits was that even though most of the interviewees expressed concern and frustration with the failure and withdrawal statistics, few faculty members saw anything out of the ordinary. One has to only imagine companies such as Motorola or General Motors accepting a product failure rate of 50 percent to realize the implication of these findings.

Clearly, bottleneck courses represent a significant impediment to student progression, with statewide implications and costs in terms of state support, student and faculty time, and facility utilization. It seems possible that distance learning technologies might help to alleviate this situation. Considering the state's access pressures, some targeted development in these critical subject areas could make a significant impact on the success rates and reduce the time required to obtain a degree.

Beyond Distance Learning

In a state that has successfully located community colleges within commuting distance of almost its entire population, the need for distance learning may not be obvious. Interviews conducted during institutional visits yielded several important insights and some interesting reactions. While the term *distance learning* is currently popular, several faculty and administrators stressed the importance of conceptualizing the issue as *technology-assisted learning*, with the understanding that even some low-tech tools such as Dictaphones and cassette players can have high impact if used as part of an overall strategy that takes individual students' strengths, weaknesses, and learning styles into account.

At Miami-Dade Community College, this is referred to as *technology-assisted, facilitated learning*. Although a large number of these technology-based initiatives are in place, documentation of their effectiveness, particularly with students who retake courses in the core disciplines, is not often readily available. Experience elsewhere suggests that the high-demand courses identified in the bottleneck analysis are particularly suited for the application of instructional technologies. In mathematics, for instance, some studies have shown that gains can be achieved in basic algebra and remedial math courses using combinations of preprogrammed problem sets that students can work through at their own pace, supported by on-line asynchronous interaction with faculty and peers (National Center for Higher Education Management Systems, 1997). Effective applications, moreover, can be both at a distance and for students currently enrolled in traditional campus-based programs. The principal positive effects reported in these studies were reduced failure and withdrawal rates. Thus these findings have implications for both the entry-level access and retention and completion problems associated with Florida's bottleneck course dilemma. Clearly, the ability of students to get in the door must be weighed against their success in exiting with the desired learning objective achieved. Distance learning technology represents much more than a conduit for accepting an ever-increasing flow of incoming students. It is potentially a launching pad for a shift from instruction based on seat time to the demonstration of learned competencies.

At a November 1995 meeting, members of the IATT project steering committee worked with math and science faculty resource groups to conceptualize the ideal use of technology in the bottleneck courses. The general picture that evolved included the following points:

- A "solution box" that could be made up of a variety of media from high school sophomore through lower-division level content.
- A subject-matter content that should have big-picture relevance for the students, and should contain elements of high touch and learning support for the students.
- A modular concept—that is, a set of modules that should be multiple-platform capable, inexpensive, and versatile.
- The modules should be used to assemble a complete course or as a part of a course.
- The modules should require day-to-day discipline and assignments.
- The modules should employ an effective placement component—both pre-course and during the course.

The work groups proposed the set of criteria as an initial conceptual basis for the effective design of any technologically delivered instruction in the mathematics and science content areas. Many of the criteria would probably seem very familiar to those involved in technologically based instruction. A significant point of difference concerns the workgroups' understanding that many of the critical skills and abilities necessary for successful completion of the targeted content areas are first presented at the high school sophomore level. In a collaborative sense, content developed for use in relieving the bottleneck pressures at the postsecondary level would be extremely useful for high school math and science courses as well as postsecondary remediation. Clearly, the instructional materials developed could address bottlenecks in math and science courses at more than one level of instruction. In this sense, the project could gain much through collaboration with all levels of education.

Collaboration and Focus on State Priorities

In a 1995 report on the status of telecommunications in Florida, the commission recommended guiding principles to focus state resources for technology on specific educational goals. First among these was that "funding requests for technologically delivered postsecondary instruction should be targeted toward courses and programs that will increase the educational system's capacity and ease current access pressures" (Statewide Telecommunications Task Force, 1995, p. 6). Also in early 1995, the Board of Regents published a supplement to the Master Plan on Distance Learning and distributed approximately $3 million for institutional distance learning demonstration projects appropriated by the 1994 legislature. Of the ten top-ranked proposals, only one addressed the issue of access to undergraduate instruction, and this was not included in the five projects funded. The 1995 legislature that met following the Regents' action did not appropriate any additional funding for distance learning. Following the legislative session, the Board of Regents and State Board of Community Colleges established a joint presidential task force to develop a unified approach to distance learning. Prominent in the budget proposal that emerged from this collaborative effort was support for projects to address the bottleneck issue identified by the commission. The 1996 legislature appropriated $15.4 million for public postsecondary distance learning initiatives but did not specify how the money was to be used. To date, approximately $1 million has been earmarked for administration and oversight and $8 million allocated for program development, an automated student advising system, and library resources. The success of this budgetary initiative can be traced to two important components. First, the collaborative nature of the request was critical. The State University System and the State Board of Community Colleges combined their efforts in a unified direction and pledged to reduce or eliminate duplication of effort. Second, the budget proposal contained areas of emphasis that were targeted toward generally accepted postsecondary priorities such as bottleneck courses, faculty and staff training, course development, and student support services. Little emphasis was placed on the acquisition of hardware. Distribution of the funds will be determined by the Florida Distance Learning Network, a statutory oversight group with representatives from education, government, and industry. A request for proposals developed and distributed by the state university and community college systems includes addressing bottleneck courses as part of an initial $3 million grant program to promote access to undergraduate degrees. The RFPs have been circulated and reviewed. All selected projects involve at least one community college and one university. Several of the successful proposals indicated priority would be given to bottleneck courses within these programs. Several software vendors have expressed interest in the bottleneck problem and at least one is actively partnering with several institutions on modification and testing of existing software packages.

Assessing Where We Are

The commission continues to work with a statewide faculty network, the Higher Education Consortium for Mathematics and Science, on the issue. Both supporters and skeptics have been recruited to assist in examining the potential of technology and distance learning on student success in bottleneck courses. In the words of one faculty member, "As we continue to apply technology to all levels of postsecondary instruction, we should be mindful that it is possible to test and definitively evaluate the effectiveness of technology that is being introduced. If we neglect to pay attention to this part of the problem, we are certain to participate in the expenditure of substantial sums with little net reward" (Ralph Dougherty, personal communication, November 30, 1995).

In spring 1996, the commission entered into another collaborative venture with a university-based project that was conducting a landscape analysis of the community college math and science curriculum, specifically algebra and biology. Survey data have been collected on the perceptions and performance of nearly fifteen hundred community college students in sections of these subjects that are taught in a traditional face-to-face format versus sections involving one or more forms of technology—laser disc, telecomputing, optical imagery scanning, or computers. Department chairs in math and science at each Florida community college were asked to designate one section as traditional from the standpoint of the instructor's use of technology in the delivery of instruction. The department chairs designated another section as nontraditional. Students in these sections were given a survey asking them to categorize the instructor's style as traditional or nontraditional, list the instructional techniques used on a regular basis in the class, and comment on their experiences with and opinions about the ability of technology to improve instruction and student learning.

The survey data have been entered and some preliminary findings have emerged. Perhaps one of the most interesting is that department chairs and students disagree as to what makes a course section nontraditional from an educational technology perspective. Two-thirds of the students in the sections designated by department chairs as nontraditional categorized the instructor's style as primarily traditional! There was greater agreement between students and department chairs concerning what makes a course traditional. Another preliminary finding is that the nontraditional classrooms look a lot like the traditional classrooms. Nontraditional sections were more likely to employ educational technology to supplement traditional instructional techniques—but not much more likely, however. Students in the nontraditional algebra sections were about 17 percent more likely to make regular use of calculators than were students in the traditional algebra sections. These survey data will be the focus of further study in the future. Perhaps the real story of the survey data is that even so-called nontraditional classrooms do not look all that nontraditional yet. Among educational technologies, the greatest difference between sections was that in the nontraditional classrooms, instructors were more likely to make use of an overhead projector.

Conclusions and Implications for Further Research

The intent of the IATT project was to seek practical applications of technology for a pressing state problem, increasing student access to postsecondary education and decreasing time-to-degree. Although work on technologically enhanced mathematics and science programs continues to be its focus, the project has brought about a number of unanticipated benefits. The data generated during the exploratory phase of the project and the focus on bottleneck courses, defined as those that students have difficulty completing, has raised the level of awareness and discussion among educational leaders and policymakers in the state. In addition, the IATT project has increased attention upon mathematics and science education, identified a practical definition and focus on degree bottlenecks, provided a focus for collaboration across the educational sectors in the development of technologically enhanced or delivered instruction, and created an opportunity for discussions concerning the reconceptualization of instruction using educational technology.

In a philosophical sense, the legislative initiatives to improve productivity and reduce time-to-degree for Florida students have involved discussions of how to break from old models of postsecondary instruction and introduce new ways to accomplish the same goals. The revenue picture for education in Florida will not improve to the point where the current instructional models based on seat time and fifteen-week semesters will adequately serve the flood of additional high school graduates seeking admission to the system. High school students entering our colleges and universities are much more comfortable with technology and expect to use it in their classes. Yet, as the community college survey data suggest, faculty and student perceptions as to what encompasses nontraditional instruction or technologically enhanced instruction appear to differ widely. Integrating educational technology into the existing curriculum is a difficult process and technology training for postsecondary faculty is also problematic. Many of our postsecondary faculty do not have access to instructional technology in the classroom beyond an overhead projector. Computers in faculty offices seem to be primarily relegated to word processing and electronic mail. The development of individualized, asynchronous alternatives to instruction such as those envisioned by this project will involve a radical reconceptualization of the traditional postsecondary instructional process. The easiest part of the project will be to employ technology to deliver instruction. The most difficult aspect will be addressing the culture of higher education and the changing work of faculty so that teaching no longer depends on the physical proximity of the student and teacher for fifteen-week semesters. Technologically enhanced or distance instructional models tend to involve more self-paced learning and be deliverable any time and any place. They have the potential to be individualized according to a student's learning style, and may involve more asynchronous faculty-student interaction. Acceptance of such concepts by the faculty is critical if educational technologies are to be effectively employed.

While the IATT project has been successful in acting as a catalyst for discussion covering a wide range of instructional and technological issues, there is much that is not known. Further analysis should be performed to determine if the pattern of failure and withdrawal rates is localized to English, mathematics, and science courses in other sectors of the State University System and within institutions and systems outside Florida. The overall efficacy of technologically delivered instruction programs and services remains in question. Some effective curricular modules designed around the IATT criteria or similar concepts need to be tested along with some models for the effective integration of technology into the postsecondary curriculum. Because of the relatively small percentage of overall coursework involved (5 percent of total offerings in Florida's community college system) and the relative transferability of such coursework to Florida or other institutions, the high-demand areas identified by the IATT project would seem to be extremely attractive targets for technological adaptation and enhancement. Serious interest from state policymakers and private software vendors suggests the potential for the development of partnerships and funding opportunities for some pilot development projects. All that is needed is a few interested institutions or faculty groups willing to dedicate some time and effort to trying to improve student learning in priority subject matter courses. Unfortunately, although many have expressed concern with the current situation, few faculty members and institutions have as yet made serious commitments to the use of distance learning technology in addressing the challenge of bottleneck courses. The future success of this technology lies in its potential to address critical state and national problems.

References

Laws of Florida, Chapter 95–243, 1995.

Miller, M. "Florida Public High School Graduates, Actual and Projected 1969–70—2010–2011." Tallahassee: Florida Department of Education, 1996.

National Center for Higher Education Management Systems. *Major Issues in Technology for Florida Postsecondary Education: An Analysis and Recommendations.* Boulder, Colo: National Center for Higher Education Management Systems, 1997.

Office of Planning and Budgeting. *Florida's Final Budget Report and Ten-Year Summary of Appropriations, 1986–87 Through 1995–96*, Vol. 18. Tallahassee, Fla.: Office of Planning and Budgeting, 1996.

Statewide Telecommunications Task Force, Florida Postsecondary Education Planning Commission. *Report and Recommendations by the Florida Postsecondary Education Planning Commission.* Tallahassee, Fla: Florida Department of Education, Dec. 1995.

Washington State Higher Education Coordinating Board. "1996–97 Tuition and Fee Rates: A National Comparison." Olympia, Wash.: Washington State Education Coordinating Board, 1997.

PATRICK DALLET *is assistant executive director of the Florida Postsecondary Education Planning Commission.*

JOHN H. OPPER *is a policy analyst with the Florida Postsecondary Education Planning Commission. He coordinates initiatives and analyses related to the development and application of distance learning technology.*

This chapter describes a framework for developing evaluation standards for distance education in statewide, multistate, and national systems, and the role of the community college in the evaluation process.

Localizing National Standards for Evaluation of Distance Education: An Example from a Multistate Project

Christine K. Sorensen

As distance education expands with the advent of new technologies, it becomes increasingly important to evaluate its use and its impact on the educational system. With the development of statewide distance education systems, evaluation takes on new dimensions. Evaluation must not only meet the needs of the local institutions, it must also serve state and sometimes federal agencies. The information demands of multiple clients may lead to complex evaluation plans, plans that ultimately affect the activities of the institutions involved. This chapter describes the development of effectiveness indicators that address the needs of local, federal, and multistate stakeholders. The community college can help by identifying local priorities, fostering new partnerships, and assisting with the collection of assessment data.

In 1987, Congress authorized an initiative, the Star Schools Program Assistance Act, to promote use of telecommunications in education. Initial funding was provided to multistate public and private consortia offering satellite instruction (Simonson, 1994; Wilson, 1990). More recently, the Star Schools program has pushed new technologies to the forefront of distance education through the funding of demonstration projects employing fiber-optic voice, video, and data transmission.

In 1992, Iowa received a special statewide Star Schools grant to demonstrate the use of fiber-optic technology to provide live two-way, full-motion interactive instruction allowing greater levels of interactivity than available in previous forms of distance instruction (Simonson, 1994). A two-year $8 million grant for development of the state's fiber-optic system was awarded to a partnership of Iowa educational institutions, which included all fifteen of Iowa's community colleges. By October 1993, 103 two-way interactive video classrooms in community colleges, universities, and K–12 schools were connected to the Iowa Communications Network (ICN) and fully operational. In 1995 and 1996, Iowa received additional Star Schools funding. Three years later, nearly 300 classrooms were operational.

Iowa's leadership in the use of distance education resulted from the state's commitment to a statewide fiber-optic system that provides for two-way full-motion video interaction as well as data transmission. The focus on two-way fiber-optic video instruction illustrates the shift in distance education to group methods of instruction that allow "sustained interaction among teacher and students" (Garrison, 1990, p. 18), similar to the traditional classroom. As Iowa became a leader in the use of two-way interactive fiber-optic technology for instructional delivery, it became important that the effectiveness of this mode of delivery be assessed so that improvements could be made and others implementing this form of technology could learn from Iowa's experience.

Community colleges have been key players in the development and evaluation of the state's distance education system. One unique challenge facing the community colleges involved in a statewide evaluation is to ensure that all educational entities in the system agree on the importance of evaluation and the indicators of success. A second challenge is to ensure consistent data collection across the state without requiring unreasonable demands on personnel at local institutions. In Iowa, a third challenge was presented with the establishment of national evaluation indicators for federally funded Star Schools projects.

In this chapter, the evaluation of Iowa's Star Schools project will be used as an example in merging evaluation criteria and collecting data on a statewide basis. First, the community college role in the development of indicators and the collection of data will be outlined. Second, the development of national evaluation indicators will be explained. The third section will present preliminary findings from Iowa. Finally, how these indicators can be used to determine local needs and describe local success will be explained.

State Evaluation Plan

Iowa is a state with a long history of local control, which helped define a singular role for the community colleges in the development of the state-funded fiber-optic system, the ICN. Iowa community colleges were connected as part of the initial backbone of the ICN system and were also responsible for selecting the sites to be connected in the second phase. In addition, community colleges are responsible for scheduling use of the system within their regions.

In most of Iowa's fifteen regions, community colleges served as the coordinating agencies for Star Schools activities from 1992 to 1994. Involvement in these activities led community colleges to develop stronger partnerships with other educational institutions in their regions, particularly with the area education agencies (AEAs) that provide assistance to local K–12 schools.

AEAs served as coordinating agencies for Iowa Star Schools activities for the 1995 phase of the project, although community colleges maintained scheduling control and provided technical assistance. In each community college region, a regional technology committee (RTC) has been formed to provide leadership and direction in the integration of technology in local education systems. RTC members represent community colleges, AEAs, and local schools, as well as state and private colleges and universities and others.

Community colleges were involved in both the development of evaluation measures for the state's distance education system and in the collection of data. Community college representatives provided feedback during initial phases of ICN use regarding indicators of success, and regional coordinators housed at community colleges were responsible for collecting and reporting data from each of the state's fifteen community college regions during the first two years of ICN operation.

Evaluation indicators were selected by the partners involved in Iowa's project. These partners included Iowa Public Television, the state's regent universities, the state's fifteen community colleges, the state's fifteen area education agencies, and the state department of education. Representatives from these groups served on a Partner's Council for the Iowa Star Schools project. The Partner's Council assisted in identifying the most important evaluation questions to ask in assessing the project's impact on distance education in the state. In addition, a Research and Evaluation Advisory Panel that included representatives of community colleges, area education agencies, regent universities, private universities, local schools, the state department of education, and the First in the Nation in Education (FINE) foundation, assisted in the development of instruments to be used in evaluation activities.

The state indicators were developed using an evaluation tool called the *a-e-I-o-u approach*, which looks at accountability, effectiveness, impact, organizational context, and unanticipated outcomes. This approach was developed and refined by James Fortune, Jan Sweeney, and Christine Sorensen, and has been used for several years by the Research Institute for Studies in Education (RISE) at Iowa State University. RISE was responsible for evaluating Iowa's Star Schools projects.

Evaluation Framework. Coldeway (1988) suggests that distance education evaluation should focus both on the need to improve (formative evaluation) as well as on describing outcomes (summative evaluation). The a-e-I-o-u approach allows for the collection of both formative and summative information and the use of both qualitative and quantitative data collection techniques. Critical in using the a-e-I-o-u approach is the involvement of stakeholders in the determination of key evaluation questions and data sources. Stakeholders are asked to use the framework to identify important evaluation questions, particularly for the accountability, effectiveness, and impact components. With the a-e-I-o-u framework as a reference, members of the Partner's Council were asked to identify indicators that could determine whether the project had accomplished its goals (accountability), how well the activities were done (effectiveness), and what difference it made for Iowa education (impact). Members of the Partner's Council as well as regional coordinators (community college personnel during the first two years of ICN operation) were also asked to identify organizational or environmental factors that either helped or hindered the project and to note unanticipated activities, events, and outcomes that occurred during the project.

Accountability questions are targeted at finding out if project objectives and activities were completed. In evaluating a distance education system, such questions might include How many classrooms were connected? How many training opportunities were provided? How many copies of developed materials were produced and distributed?

Effectiveness questions are directed at placing value on the project's activities. They generally focus on participant attitudes and knowledge. Grades and achievement tests are effectiveness measures, as are attitude and perception information gathered through surveys or focus groups. Effectiveness questions might include Did teachers feel adequately prepared to teach over a distance? How well did students learn? Were students, faculty, and administrators satisfied with distance education opportunities and experiences? Did users of developed software rate the product positively?

Impact questions are aimed at identifying changes in the behavior of individuals, groups, or systems. Data sources include record data, surveys, policy analyses, interviews, focus groups, and direct observation. Did classroom use increase? Did demands for access increase? Were more educational institutions involved in technology planning?

Organizational context questions focus on identifying contextual or environmental factors, policies, or events beyond the control of the participants that contributed to or detracted from the project. Methods of data collection include interviews of key personnel, focus groups, and document analyses designed to identify policies and procedures that influence the program. Organizational context questions might include What factors made it difficult to implement the project? What did participants think contributed most to the success of the project?

Unanticipated outcomes questions attempt to identify unexpected changes of either a positive or negative nature that occur as a result of the project. Like impact questions, these questions are directed at identifying changes in behavior of individuals, organizations, or systems through examination of data collected through interviews, focus groups, observations, and surveys. Often, evaluators must interact with project participants to learn about unplanned successes and failures that result from a project. Informal communication and observation are useful methods to gather this information. Questions might include Was the distance education system used in unexpected ways? Did relationships between collaborators change in unexpected ways?

State Indicators. In Iowa, statewide indicators of distance education success were selected using the a-e-I-o-u approach. The primary emphases in the development of distance education in the state since 1992 can be summarized as: (1) expanding access to education through the development of a distance education infrastructure, (2) training and involving current and future educators in the use of distance education, (3) informing the public and coordinating the use of distance education in the state, and (4) supporting effective distance instruction and developing effective instructional materials for distance use. For each of these goals, indicators were identified to assess accountability, effectiveness, and impact. Accountability indicators assessed number of sites, training opportunities, and programs, as well as information dissemination; effectiveness indicators addressed user satisfaction; and impact indicators assessed use, demand, and diffusion. In addition, project participants were asked to report their perceptions of organizational and environmental factors that helped or hindered the project and any unanticipated outcomes that resulted from project activities. Encouraging participants to be aware of the context can help in overcoming obstacles and in developing an understanding of the factors that affect the ability of a project to accomplish its goals. Awareness of unanticipated outcomes can also assist in future planning efforts and aid in further understanding of potential consequences of decisions.

Adapting to National Expectations

Iowa was the first, but not the only, statewide distance education project funded through the Star Schools program. In 1994, Kentucky received funding to develop a statewide system, and in 1995, Mississippi received funding. The Iowa, Kentucky, and Mississippi Star Schools projects are referred to as the "special statewide projects." These projects are unusual in the Star Schools program, a program that has traditionally focused on satellite delivery of distance instruction, because of their emphasis on developing statewide infrastructures for distance education. A set of indicators was developed by the Star Schools program to evaluate the satellite-based projects nationwide, based on program goals. Because of the differences among the projects, evaluators and project directors from the three statewide projects felt that some modifications in the federal indicators were needed, and in early 1996, they agreed upon a set of revised indicators to measure their success. These indicators were approved by the federal Star Schools project in March, 1996.

- *Goal 1: To increase access to educational programs by establishing a technological infrastructure.* Indicators addressed number of sites, infrastructure connections, lines and bandwidth available, and data connections proved.
- *Goal 2: To reach underserved learners throughout the United States and its affiliated territories.* Indicators addressed characteristics of connected sites, usage, and demographic characteristics of participating students.
- *Goal 3: To expand instruction in core subject areas as well as literacy skills and vocational education.* Indicators assessed the program activities by subject area, teacher perceptions of improved skills, and student satisfaction.
- *Goal 4: To provide professional development that is sustained over a period of time.* Indicators examined number of participants, satisfaction, impact upon practice, impact upon demand, and evidence of continuation.

- *Goal 5: To employ a variety of electronic technologies and tools for distance education.* Indicators assessed the type and number of technologies, accessibility of technology, and institutional usage.
- *Goal 6: To foster partnerships.* Indicators addressed the number of partnerships, the role of the partners, and the incidents of collaboration.
- *Goal 7: To demonstrate improved cost-benefit ratios.* Indicators identified fixed and variable costs ratios and assessed the value of expanded access.

Since data concerning the national indicators is required for Iowa's Star Schools project, it was critical that these indicators be incorporated into Iowa's already comprehensive evaluation plan. In many cases, the indicators developed through Iowa's evaluation process were consistent with the national indicators. Indicators from the state and national plans were combined within the a-e-I-o-u framework, using the national goals as a base and incorporating state goals related to information coordination. The resulting set of indicators includes accountability indicators, effectiveness indicators, and impact indicators.

Summary of Preliminary Findings

This summary of preliminary findings is meant only to provide some sense of the information gathered. Extensive reporting of methodologies and results is beyond the scope of this chapter. More detailed information can be obtained from individual studies and project evaluation reports (Sorensen, 1995; Sorensen and Sweeney, 1994; Sorensen, Maushak, and Lozada, 1996).

Infrastructure Development. Goal 1 involved development of the state's distance education infrastructure. By June 1996, ninety interactive television classrooms were located in K–12 schools, fifty-two in community colleges, twenty-four at public universities and AEAs, and thirty-seven at other locations. Equipment was purchased to connect the ICN to other networks and to allow the delivery of multimedia products from remote servers. Surveys of teachers and students at the K–12 and community college levels showed satisfaction with distance education experiences. While most institutions were satisfied with the distribution of funds, some dissatisfaction was expressed about connection delays. ICN use increased from sixteen thousand hours in fall 1994 to fifty-six thousand hours in spring 1996. K–12 schools accounted for about 25 percent of the system use, while higher education, primarily community colleges, accounted for 60 percent. Regional coordinators reported increased demand for ICN and Internet connections and indicated that the project had motivated schools to adopt and use a variety of technologies much sooner than they would have otherwise.

Underserved Learners. Goal 2 was to reach underserved learners. As a result of the project, 33 percent of the school districts classified as Chapter One concentration sites have access to an ICN classroom, as do over 25 percent of the school districts where more than one-third of students qualified for free or reduced-price lunches, 63 percent of districts with concentrations of minority students, 77 percent of districts with concentrations of students with limited English proficiency, and 38 percent of districts in high-poverty counties (where more than 20 percent of seventeen-year-olds and younger live in poverty). School districts participating in courses offered over the ICN during spring 1996 included twenty-eight Chapter One concentration sites, eighteen districts with minority concentrations, eleven districts with concentrations of students with limited English proficiency, thirty-seven districts with one-fourth or more of the students qualifying for free or reduced-price lunches, and twelve districts in counties with high poverty rates.

Instruction. Goal 3 was to expand instruction. Courses offered over the ICN tripled from fall 1993 to fall 1995. In addition, the system was used to provide hundreds (over seven hundred in one semester) of one-time educational events. Additional analysis of scheduling information is under way to determine participation in instructional activities and courses by subject area, audience, and educational level. Early surveys of teachers and students at both the K–12 and community college levels indicate that both groups are satisfied with the delivery method and with the instruction received. In addition, ratings indicate a belief that distance education instruction is effective. Comparison of community college student grade point averages showed no differences between students at remote and origination sites (where the teacher was physically present). Additional surveys of students and teachers are scheduled. Thirty-five school districts initiated grant-funded projects to adapt their curriculum to incorporate technology. Regional coordinators reported increased use of technology in the schools as well as changes in the curriculum resulting from the projects. Coordinators also reported increased access to learning opportunities for both students and staff in the regions.

Professional Development and Support. Goal 4 was to provide professional development and support for educators to use distance education. During the project, numerous local opportunities for staff development in the use of technology, including training in the use of the ICN and Internet, were provided across the state. Surveys of participants indicate that these staff development activities were worthwhile. Pre and post surveys of training participants showed knowledge gains. Regional coordinators also reported an increase in the number of staff development opportunities available over the ICN and higher participation rates, attributed in part to convenience and savings in time and money that individual teachers and districts realize through taking advantage of staff development at a distance. AEAs reported increased abilities to offer in-service opportunities to teachers through use of the ICN. Help desk and room manager training sessions were also held, as were sessions on developing local and wide area networks. Participants rated these sessions as effective. Regional coordinators reported increased requests for assistance with technology planning and technical support. Workshops were also held for faculty at colleges involved in teacher training.

Electronic Technologies. Goal 5 was to support the development and use of a variety of distance learning technologies. The project was successful in assisting education institutions in obtaining equipment for use in ICN video classrooms and to connect to the Internet. Six proposals were funded to develop multimedia instructional materials for a variety of educational levels in a variety of content areas: two from community colleges, two from AEAs, one from a public university, and one from a local school district. Also, 278 examples of technology for teaching were identified. Nineteen were selected as exemplary applications, including four for higher education and fifteen for K–12. Showcases were held to demonstrate these exemplary applications to other teachers. Follow-up studies will assess perceptions of users of the multimedia products.

Partnerships. Goal 6 was to develop partnerships among educational institutions. Of the variety of groups involved, several have representation on the leadership committee for the project. Regional coordinators have reported improvements in collaboration among educational organizations within the region, especially between community colleges and AEAs, and increased sharing and cooperation among schools and across educational levels. Activities of the project have also fostered partnerships and collaboration among preservice teacher education programs across the state.

Costs and Benefits. Goal 7 was to improve the cost-benefit ratio for distance education. The Iowa project initially began comparing costs for alternative activities. Based on these initial analyses, regional coordinators report savings in time and travel costs for teachers through use of ICN in-service activities. Although these analyses were a beginning, the evaluators have a goal of defining additional cost analysis measures and procedures. For instance, benefits such as the value of increased access to educational programming of this system cannot be measured purely in terms of dollars saved.

Information Coordination. Goal 8 was to provide coordination of information about distance education in the state. The Iowa Database site on the World Wide Web continues to grow, with recent additions including a PBS series, information on exemplary applications of technology, a searchable list of ICN classes, and a clickable map of ICN sites. Use of the database has increased from two hundred files transmitted per day in fall 1995 to six hundred per day in spring 1996. The monthly number of files accessed has risen from about five thousand to nearly twenty thousand. Both educational and commercial users offer positive ratings. Brochures, pamphlets, and videos were developed and have been distributed statewide. Nearly fifteen thousand Iowans attended demonstrations of the ICN and 76 percent reported feeling it would benefit students in the state and provide increased access to resources. In addition, an encyclopedia of research on distance education in Iowa was completed and distributed.

Local Needs and Local Success

By involving all segments of the educational community in determining the indicators for evaluating distance education in the state, individual institutions become more willing to use the findings to improve local initiatives. Individual institutions are able to see areas of strength as well as areas for improvement. For instance, institutions can take a closer look at distance education services to schools in their region with high percentages of underserved students. Instruments used to assess student and teacher attitudes toward distance education activities can be used by the community college to investigate ways to increase satisfaction. Involving all stakeholders in defining evaluation indicators helps to ensure that indicators of local importance are incorporated into the larger evaluation plan. Consistency in data collection across institutions both ensures that data can be combined to look at the larger picture and enables comparisons to be made. The ability to see where an individual institution stands in relationship to the state allows benchmarking to occur.

Individual institutions can use the a-e-I-o-u framework, evaluation measures, and data collection strategies developed for the statewide evaluation in a number of ways. The statewide plan provides a coherent structure for evaluation of distance education in a variety of settings. Although individual institutions may not want to invest the resources necessary to implement measurement of all the indicators discussed in the Iowa plan, the framework developed for the statewide evaluation is useful in providing direction and insights into ways to evaluate distance education.

Measures outlined under accountability could be used in developing plans to assess the growth and development of local infrastructure, document the use of the local system, document the constituencies served, document staff development opportunities provided and attendance trends, and document courses and educational opportunities provided and attendance trends. These are all important areas to look at in evaluating local use of distance education and in planning for future distance education initiatives.

Effectiveness measures described in the statewide plan are also useful at the local level. Individual institutions might want to use similar indicators in efforts to improve the quality of distance education programs locally. Effectiveness measures could help institutions to assess faculty and student satisfaction with courses and opportunities, measure the satisfaction of local constituents with distance education, assess technology awareness levels of faculty and students, assess satisfaction with staff development provided, measure learning outcomes in a technology-mediated environment, and assess the level of access to and consistency of information provided about distance education.

While accountability and effectiveness are important components in evaluating distance education, the bottom line for most institutions is impact. What difference has distance education made? Iowa's impact measures could be used by local institutions to measure changes in faculty behavior related to distance education, assess levels of technology integration in departments and units, measure levels of use of technology and instructional products, and assess the costs and benefits of distance education for the individual institution.

Individual institutions may also define important factors that have helped or hindered them in creating an effective distance education delivery system by looking critically at the organizational context. By focusing attention on the local context, institutions may become more aware of internal technology planning initiatives, increase collaboration within the institution, and provide avenues for increased coordination of efforts.

By making it explicit, the a-e-I-o-u framework focuses attention on the possibility of unanticipated outcomes occurring, a useful concept. Unintended consequences are often overlooked, although they might provide some valuable lessons. Positive outcomes may be ignored because evaluators are looking for something else, and the institution is then unable to take advantage of or build upon these outcomes. If unforeseen negative outcomes are ignored, strategies for dealing with them may not be developed. Outcomes can be unpredictable and conscious awareness of that fact is a first step in benefiting from unforeseen positive consequences and averting or correcting negative ones.

The a-e-I-o-u framework that was developed and refined as part of the Iowa Star Schools project can be a useful tool for community colleges. Not only can the framework be useful in designing evaluation plans for distance education, but also for designing evaluations for a variety of projects or programs. It is a framework that was adapted in Iowa to work in a statewide context, but it is also one that community colleges can use to address local needs and evaluate local success.

References

Coldeway, D. O. "Methodological Issues in Distance Education Research." *The American Journal of Distance Education,* 1988, 2 (3), 36–44.

Garrison, D. R. "An Analysis and Evaluation of Audio Teleconferencing to Facilitate Education at a Distance." *American Journal of Distance Education,* 1990, 4 (3), 13–24.

Simonson, M. "Two-Way Interactive Distance Education: Iowa's Star Schools Project." *Educational IRM Quarterly,* 1994, 3 (2), 10–13.

Sorensen, C. "Evaluation of Interactive Television Instruction: Assessing Attitudes of Community College Students." *DEOSNEWS: The Electronic Journal on Distance Education,* October, 1995, 5 (9). [Archived at listserv@psuvm.psu.edu, command: get deosnews 95–00009.]

Sorensen, C., and Sweeney, J. *Iowa Distance Education Alliance: Final Evaluation Report.* Ames, Iowa: Research Institute for Studies in Education, 1994.

Sorensen, C., Maushak, N., and Lozada, M. *Iowa Distance Education Alliance Evaluation Report: Fall 1995–Spring 1996.* Ames, Iowa: Research Institute for Studies in Education, 1996.

Wilson, B. "Students' Assessment of Distance Learning." Paper presented at the annual meeting of the Mid-South Educational Research Association, New Orleans, La., 1990. (ED 326 558)

CHRISTINE K. SORENSEN *is currently an assistant professor in the College of Education at Northern Illinois University. From 1992 to 1996, she was an evaluation specialist at Iowa State University and was responsible for coordinating evaluation activities for a variety of technology-related projects, including a statewide distance education initiative.*

This chapter examines the wide variety of new issues arising for community colleges participating in virtual universities, whether as providers of instruction or student support services.

Implications of a Virtual University for Community Colleges

Sally M. Johnstone, Stephen Tilson

Dozens of virtual universities have been born in the 1990s—some organized by existing corporations in the electronics or telecommunications industry (International University by Jones Cable), some formed as independent start-up institutions (Magellan University out of Arizona), and some emerging from consortia of existing institutions (Colorado Electronic Community College). While virtual universities may take many forms, this chapter focuses primarily on one: the Western Governors University (WGU) and how it can affect the role of the community college.

The WGU sprang from a June 1995 annual meeting of the Western Governors Association, where discussion centered on technology and higher education. Utah Governor Mike Leavitt suggested that western universities avoid duplication of distance learning courses and collaborate in the development and delivery of courses. Colorado Governor Roy Romer added the idea of measuring, assessing, and certifying competencies and learning.

At their meeting in late fall 1995, the western governors appointed a design team and charged it with the responsibility of creating a design plan for a virtual university to serve the western region and an implementation plan through which such an entity could be established and financed. The educational members of this design team were from the staff of two organizations in Boulder, Colorado: the National Center for Higher Education Management Systems (NCHEMS) and the Western Cooperative for Educational Telecommunications, a project of the Western Interstate Commission for Higher Education (WICHE).

The governors asked that the institution be designed to facilitate the widespread use of technologically delivered educational programming offering

New Directions for Community Colleges, no. 99, Fall 1997 © Jossey-Bass Publishers certification through competency assessment. They outlined the following design parameters (which can be obtained through the Western Governors University Web site, which is listed in the resources at the end of this chapter):

The institution will be *market-oriented* and *client-centered*. The governors want an institution that is both flexible and responsive to the changing needs of the citizens and employers in their states. While they do not propose that a student design his or her own curriculum, they want students to be able to navigate easily through the systems and requirements of the institution. They want an institution with a service orientation.

The institution will be *degree-granting* and *accredited* by the appropriate academic associations. The degrees granted by the institution will be *competency-based* rather than based on the accumulation of credit hours related to seat-time. It is the student's skills and knowledge that will be credentialed, not the qualifications of the people designing, developing, or delivering the learning opportunities.

The institution will have a *distributed teaching faculty* who will come from public and private higher education institutions, as well as from private industry.

The institution will achieve *cost-effectiveness* through the sharing of *regional* resources. Translating courses and whole academic programs into an electronic environment is expensive, and to have each institution within a state replicate what its sister institutions are already doing would be a waste of resources. The institution can serve as a vehicle for both intra- and inter-state sharing of resources for cooperative development of electronically delivered academic programs.

It must be *initiated quickly*. The official planning began in January 1996 and the institution was incorporated in January 1997. It is expected to be operational by January 1998.

The governors further recommended that the WGU carry out its mission by focusing on those areas where it can most effectively add value to existing initiatives and capacity. On this basis, the WGU should:

Link employers and academic institutions in setting skills standards, link individuals seeking assessment of their competencies with assessment providers, and certify competence in several domains of learning—transferable skills (communication, quantitative reasoning, etc.), vocational skills, general academic knowledge, and specific disciplinary knowledge.

Link individuals seeking to enhance their level of competence in one or more of these areas with providers of educational programs, courses, or modules who can meet the learners' requirements regarding time, place, and content of services delivered.

Provide support services needed to help ensure that students receive appropriate guidance and that barriers to access to educational offerings are minimized or removed entirely.

Gather the financial resources needed to develop learning modules and assessment tools in high-priority areas, and in which the market has not already responded.

Provide credentials to individuals—academic degrees and industry-recognized workplace certificates—based on assessment of competencies.

In summary, this collaborative virtual university is being formed to facilitate the use of existing institutional resources by making them more accessible to students. One of the tools used to accomplish this is a unique method of earning credentials that removes the usual institutional barriers that arise with multiple institutions in an electronic environment. The WGU will also help streamline student support services by using local centers at existing institutions such as public libraries, small businesses, and community colleges.

Quality Assurance

The WGU, like other virtual university frameworks, must make some critical decisions to ensure quality. Since the teaching faculty will be distributed across many types of institutions and many states, the WGU must have some mechanism for determining the quality of the learning experience for the student. While a centralized group can never monitor or even coordinate the monitoring of a multistate system, the WGU can at least ensure that the institution or organization from which the learning experience originates is reputable and adheres to principles of good practice for electronically delivered programs. Such principles (Western Interstate Commission for Higher Education, 1995) require the institution to examine and document its support for the student who is not physically present on the campus. They also require an examination of the support the institution offers its faculty involved in teaching students electronically.

Another key factor in controlling the quality of the teaching and learning environment is the emphasis on measurable outcomes. WGU degrees and certificates will be based on assessments of a student's skills and knowledge, not on the number of hours spent in a classroom. In addition, all the coursework offered through the WGU will include information on skills and knowledge expected to be acquired as a result of taking a particular course. The WGU will track the success rates of students in each of the learning options on WGU assessments and make these public. This will allow prospective students to make course choices based on how useful other students have found a particular learning option to be in actually aiding in the development of the knowledge and skills the course purports to offer.

For example, let us assume a student is seeking a WGU certificate in Electronic Manufacturing Technology (EMT). She could find out about the certificate option and other WGU information in one of three ways:

• Going into the WGU smart catalogue and adviser Web site directly from her own computer

- Visiting a local center and using its computer links or talking with a person there who would consult the Web site
- Calling a toll-free number and talking with an adviser who is linked to the Web site

She would first be given information on the specific skills and knowledge she would need to demonstrate to be awarded the EMT certificate. By participating in an on-line self-assessment of her current level of skills and knowledge in this area, she would be able to define what areas are most critical in her preparation. She could then search through a menu of course options from different institutions and organizations. Each option would include information that could help her make a choice among them:

- The skills and knowledge needed before taking the course
- The skills and knowledge the provider claims the course teaches
- The probability of actually acquiring the skills and knowledge listed above based on the assessment records of previously enrolled students
- The technologies used in the course
- The cost of the course
- How to get further information electronically about the teaching institution

The student would be able to make her choice—what course to take, and from which institution—based on the information most critical for her. She would also be able to register for that course on-line and receive very specific instructions regarding her next steps (things like how to order a book, when to contact her instructor, and so on).

This scenario offers a somewhat unusual public information approach to quality control. However, in a setting where the teaching faculty may never get to know one another and where the institutional standards may vary across different states, it is one of the few possible options open for a cooperative virtual university model.

Distributed Student Services. In many of the western states, the community colleges are the natural first tier of local centers. They are already engaged in serving local constituencies and have well-developed student support systems. However, the development of distributed student services is at least as complex as the development of new instructional methods, and as full of implications for dramatic change for the community college.

Perhaps the most pivotal part of this transition rests with the staff who typically interact directly with students on important administrative and academic matters. These support staff will have to become accustomed to dealing with students they may never meet in person. This adjustment represents as big a conceptual shift as that required of instructors in the new electronically mediated learning environment. On-line forms of registration, enrollment, and assessment testing will need to be evaluated and adopted. Bookstore staff will need to mail larger numbers of texts and other materials efficiently, as well as handle billing at a distance. With greater use of and reliance on technology, the training, orientation, and technical support for student services staff also become more important. The nature of telecommunications and the realities of modern student needs and expectations dictate that support staff adopt more of a one-stop approach to their functions. This means cross-training, with more staff learning all aspects of support services.

Virtual University Role. While campuses will want to develop some of these services internally, part of the role of the virtual university can be to remove some of the responsibility for supporting students. The WGU is designing a centralized student support system that students can use through a toll-free phone number or directly on-line. However, since these resources will not be supported in the way campus services are, students may have to pay for some of them.

Another role of the community college within the virtual university framework may be to offer support services to virtual university students living nearby and taking courses from other institutions. Inevitably, some students will prefer, even when services can be delivered directly to their home or workplace, to travel to a physical location for learning. Some learning experiences, like some students, will demand synchronous group interaction. This means the college will need to develop relationships with other institutions, in many cases institutions that are geographically far removed and quite dissimilar in size, mission, and resources. These kinds of relationships can involve familiar things like informal networks of test proctoring locations or existing articulation agreements; they can also be more complex.

Many of the mechanisms that have been used for decades simply do not apply to the new kinds of collaboration required by this distributed situation. There are still no broadly accepted models regarding who pays whom for what. The WGU designers recognize the need to have local service providers reimbursed for their efforts, but at this writing the formula for revenue sharing has not been set.

Another key challenge involves the changing roles of the college workforce. Community college administrators must recognize the need to develop a new paraprofessional staff to serve students. Some faculty may continue to focus on designing instruction, while others will decide to specialize in particular support services, like advising. While some of these transitions are already under way, the advent of the virtual university is likely to accelerate the process.

Student Financial Aid. One student service that is particularly complex and troubling is financial aid. Traditionally, student financial aid is based in a home institution that is responsible for establishing and verifying student need and levels of support, as well as providing all required record keeping and correspondence. All money provided for the student actually goes to and is distributed by this home institution. This model is predicated on the assumption that the student is taking courses at only one institution, and that institution is local.

Several solutions for distant students and students engaged in study at multiple institutions have emerged. The simplest one is an agreement among the colleges involved, whereby one is designated the home institution for financial aid purposes. It agrees to reimburse the others at an appropriate level for services rendered. When the Colorado community college system created the Colorado Electronic Community College (CECC) to facilitate service to distant students, a special agreement was entered into between CECC and one of the existing system colleges to make an existing college the home institution for financial aid and other student service functions. This works, but obviously will be too cumbersome to use on the large-scale basis that emerges as virtual universities develop.

The real long-term response to these challenges must come from systemic policy change. In the case of financial aid, the federal government is the source of most financial aid, and sets the policies regarding its distribution. The federal agencies involved are considering, cautiously but seriously, changes in these basic policies that eventually will shift the way this system works. It seems likely that any immediate changes will be minor modifications of current practices to lessen the inequities for distant students. In the longer term, it may be that financial aid would go directly to students, rather than institutions, allowing students the flexibility to take courses wherever and however best suits them.

Costs. Institutions are faced with new or increased costs in several areas as they move into a distributed learning environment. At the least, traditional services will need to have extended hours, and this equates to higher staffing costs. New technology has to be paid for, and after the up-front purchase price, there will be ongoing costs for maintenance, connectivity, and training and orientation. On the conceptual level, as more of an institution's activities are conducted via technology, the costs of maintaining and running the physical plant can be reduced. Staff can be retrained in at least some cases, but few traditional institutions will be able to start shutting down buildings any time in the near future, so these new costs will have to be met with new sources of funding. One of the hallmarks of distributed learning is that political borders cease to have any necessary relevance. Since it seems unlikely that state legislatures or local boards of commissioners will agree to disburse taxpayer dollars to support learners in other states, a new funding mechanism must be created, perhaps by incorporating the concept of uncoupling instruction from support services.

Institutions providing noninstructional services to students might be paid for those services directly by students. This arrangement would require some careful reexamination of costs by institutions, but would benefit students in the sense that they would have a clearer understanding of exactly what their fees were paying for, and of buying only what they need. Or service costs might be covered by the originating institution, as part of the services agreement. Alternatively, student services might become part of the package provided by some brokering entity like the WGU, and covered by fees students pay to that entity. Some hybrid system could also evolve that includes aspects of each of these arrangements.

There are other ways in which a local institution might benefit by providing services to students not enrolled in a program at that college. This was demonstrated in a recent Western Cooperative for Educational Telecommunications project funded by the U.S. Department of Commerce's Telecommunications and Information Infrastructure Assistance Program. The Western Brokering Project linked specialized community college programs with students in several states, making it possible for students enrolled in a distance course to use a local college's library and technology resources. This frequently resulted in the participating student signing up for additional courses locally. Colleges found they were able to offer additional educational opportunities to their local community for minimal additional costs.

Any discussion of the costs arising from this new educational environment should include some mention of a planning process for meeting those costs. Traditional planning tools may or may not have validity. Enrollment planning, for example, will certainly change as the potential student market for a course or program shifts from a local geographical area to a much larger, interest- or need-based audience. Traditional budgeting practices generally do not allow for the kinds of investment in technology or equipment necessary and are not typically set up to cover the three-year life span of modern computer hardware. Many institutions are considering or implementing new planning processes, designed to try to meet these new imperatives. Models for planning will vary considerably from institution to institution, but any successful process will be as inclusive of various groups and needs as possible, reflect the goals and mission of the institution, and allow for flexibility to respond to quickly changing conditions.

Role of the Community College in Course Delivery

As any college takes on the responsibility of serving students that do not come to its campus, it must develop ways to support those students. It also must have sufficient institutional commitment to support its staff and faculty in their efforts to support those non–campus-based students. Working in a virtual university context can make some of this student support a little less daunting. Colleges have the opportunity to rely on a central virtual university staff to assist with student services, and they also have the chance to form partnerships with colleges in other states.

Partnerships in Course Delivery. Just as collaboration among institutions will be a central part of the new distributed learning environment with regard to student services, it will also be part of course delivery. Avoiding duplicate offerings and maximizing the effective use of resources was one of the central motivating factors behind the creation of the Western Governors University.

The idea of forging partnerships for specific purposes is certainly not new for higher education institutions, especially in the field of distance or distributed learning. Collaborating in the scheduling of telecourse broadcasts, for example, was a natural early development. This led easily to collaborating on telecourse licensing and to group buyouts of telecourse rights. The use of synchronous technologies for course delivery, whether computer, audio, or video based, demands cooperative scheduling of equipment, support staff, and rooms. The development of high-quality, high-tech curricular materials is typically beyond the existing budget of most community colleges, so joint development projects are becoming more common. These sometimes take the form of state- or system-level production facilities or operations, like Colorado's Educational Technology and Training Center or the Washington state community college system's Communications Technology Center.

The logical extension of collaborative instructional activities is the sharing of instructors among institutions. Though this is not new, it has become more feasible with the advent of technology-based teaching, which makes the physical location of the instructor mostly irrelevant.

Unique Interstate Considerations. There are several special challenges to serving students in different states. Using a virtual university framework, some of these can be made easier to overcome. Before we review these, we must acknowledge that some states still have geographic service areas. This anachronistic concept is completely unworkable and costly in an era of serving students electronically. These policies can actually discourage colleges from serving their own state citizens and encourage them to go out of state for students.

One of the trickiest aspects of interstate delivery for community colleges is what to charge out-of-state students. Since most community colleges were designed to serve their local geographic area, they do not have tuition policies that allow them to be competitive in a regional, national, or international environment. At one Colorado community college, inquiries have come in from all around the globe regarding the on-line classes they offer. They have to charge full out-of-state tuition for distant students, which makes this lower-cost learning experience too expensive for many. One proposal under discussion for the WGU is to loosen state regulations regarding charges to nonlocal students.

In addition to the challenges posed by state regulations on tuition rates, many states also require out-of-state course providers to be licensed in the state where the student resides. The requirements and procedures differ by state, which makes compliance by a virtual university program even more difficult. Researching the requirements, paying the requested fees, and filling out the appropriate documents takes staff time that typical colleges do not have to spare. Consequently, even when a good electronically delivered program may be in demand, a small college may be discouraged from offering it beyond its local area. Working in a collaborative regional organization like the WGU, reciprocal arrangements can be made among states that allow a college to comply with one set of entrance requirements applicable in all states.

Another sticky issue for colleges and the students they serve electronically is articulation, or, more often, the lack of it. More and more states are encouraging or requiring their colleges and universities to develop articulation agreements. These are rare among institutions in different states. Consequently a student who studies with multiple colleges electronically may be faced with the overwhelming burden of finding one college that will accept the courses offered by all the others. The WGU solution to the articulation dilemma is to offer the student a WGU degree, based not on the number of courses taken but rather on the skills and knowledge demonstrated as a result of taking all the courses from the various institutions.

Multiregional Accreditation. The thirteen states involved in the WGU include three different regional academic accreditation agencies: the North Central Association, the Northwest Association, and the Western Association. If a college accredited by the Northwest Association offers classes to students residing in a state typically covered by the North Central Association, who is responsible for academic quality issues? In conversations between the designers of the WGU and the executive directors of the accrediting associations, it was agreed to explore developing a procedure for multiregional accreditation. While this is an obvious solution, it has never been successful in the past. However, now seems to be the right time for exploring new ways to solve these problems.

Implications for the Future

There are two major areas in which community colleges can continue to play an integral role in the expanding influence of virtual universities. The first area involves the decision to function as a *sending institution,* providing instruction to students electronically. In this case the definition of community shifts from a geographic base to a service or academic specialization base. Few colleges (or universities for that matter) can afford to shift *all* their academic programs to this environment. Consequently, college administrators and faculty making strategic decisions about where to focus their resources should try to build on the programmatic strengths of their institution. This means that colleges will also want to be linked with others that can fill in gaps in their offerings.

The second area of consideration involves the college's position as a *student access and service center* within a virtual university. A community college can become a one-stop educational shopping center for its local constituency. This does not mean the college is a passive importer of courseware from other providers that may or may not meet its constituency's needs. There are a number of ways in which community colleges can have a powerful voice in the development of virtual universities:

- *Data Collection.* Community colleges serving as local centers will collect data to track student use and student satisfaction with imported materials. This information can be collected centrally and used to modify learning materials.
- *Local Needs Assessment.* Community colleges can identify emerging needs for particular education or training programs in specific areas to better serve their local community. The assessment of needs at a local level will help central virtual university staff in developing new programs, products, and services.

- *Marketing.* Community colleges will serve an important role in the local marketing of virtual university programs and recruitment of students.

The transformation of the community college into a local education service center for the virtual university implies the reordering and refocusing of many traditional systems and mechanisms. On the one hand, instruction, especially in niche-market specialty programs, will originate from the college. This will compel the development of new instructional methods and new services for distant students, and new collaborative relationships with other institutions. At the same time, the community college will be serving local students as their service provider—their "place to learn"—enriching the learning experience regardless of where the instruction may originate. This implies the inevitable uncoupling of instruction from student support. As instruction increasingly becomes distributed, originating elsewhere than at the local campus, the various support services and how they are paid for will have to evolve as well.

In summary, the regional virtual university, in partnership with local community colleges, will serve an essential purpose in a new higher education environment by brokering service agreements, providing models, and facilitating communication. The changes required by this transition will be dramatic, complex, and no doubt often uncomfortable—but will ultimately result in broader access to higher quality learning experiences.

Reference

Western Interstate Commission for Higher Education. *When Distance Education Crosses State Boundaries: Western States Policies 1995.* Boulder, Colo.: Western Interstate Commission for Higher Education, 1995.

Resources

Dixon, P. *Virtual College.* Princeton, N.J.: Peterson's Guide, 1996.
Distance Learning. Princeton, N.J.: Peterson's Guide, 1997.
Western Governors University Web site: http://wga-internet.westgov.org/smart/vu/vu.html.
Western Interstate Commission for Higher Education. "Principles of Good Practice for Electronically Offered Academic Degree and Certificate Programs." [http://www.wiche.edu]. June 1996.

SALLY M. JOHNSTONE is director of the Western Cooperative for Educational Telecommunications, founded in 1989 by the Western Interstate Commission for Higher Education (WICHE) in Boulder, Colorado. She is also a member of the design and implementation teams for the Western Governors University.

STEPHEN TILSON is director of distance learning at Front Range Community College in Colorado. He has served as chair of the Telecommunications Cooperative for Colorado, and of the Public Two-Year Caucus of the Western Cooperative for Educational Telecommunications.

This chapter reviews the current status of accrediting agency policies and addresses the challenges facing the organizations that evaluate and review American community colleges.

Who Sets the Standards?
Accreditation and Distance Learning

Barbara Gellman-Danley

The proliferation of distance learning courses and programs poses an enormous challenge to those agencies charged with the responsibility for accrediting community colleges. This chapter addresses how this new form of learning affects accreditation of community colleges offering distance learning programs. For the purposes of this chapter, *distance learning* is defined as "a system and a process that connects learners with distributed learning resources" (Sullivan and Rocco, 1996, p. 1).

The founding premise of community colleges is access, providing open admissions to hundreds of thousands of learners each year. Distance learning expands the traditional definition of access. Through technology, colleges can provide access to higher education beyond the confines of the campus. For accrediting agencies charged with the oversight of standards and mission compliance, this expanded access poses a whole new set of challenges for which existing guidelines are often not adequate.

As distance learning courses and programs become more numerous, community college leaders and accreditors are faced with the challenge of assuring quality. Interestingly, critics of distance learning would place distance programs under greater scrutiny in some cases than traditional on-campus programs, and accrediting agencies may apply similar standards. For some, there is a preconception that distance learning programs are inherently inferior. Although this view is rooted mostly in perception, accreditors are escalating their own reviews and standards of good practice for programs delivered away from campus. In some cases, these standards are not reinforced, or differ dramatically from state policies. Often the standards are based upon precedents that are not appropriate for new forms of delivery.

Community colleges are accredited by regional agencies as well as specialized or professional bodies in specific disciplines, such as health education programs. And while the standards are usually no different for community colleges than for senior-level institutions, it is important that community colleges keep abreast of this changing accreditation environment. This chapter reports the findings of a study of the current status of accrediting agency policies and standards for community colleges and distance learning.

Background

In 1985, the Council on Postsecondary Accreditation (COPA) and the State Higher Education Executive Officers (SHEEO) produced a study designed to provide suggestions for guidelines and oversight of distance learning. This study, Project ALLTEL: Assessing Long Distance Learning Via Telecommunications (Chaloux, 1985), is described briefly in Chapters Three and Ten. The late president of COPA, Richard M. Millard, informed the author of this chapter that several states studied and used parts of the recommendations contained in the ALLTEL study. In addition, he felt the substance of the document provided an excellent beginning to an ongoing, in-depth review of existing guidelines and their relevance to nontraditional programs.

However, national guidelines for accrediting agencies did not follow for several years. COPA was dissolved in 1993, as was its successor, the Commission on Recognition of Postsecondary Accreditation (CORPA). In March 1996, the Council for Higher Education Accreditation (CHEA) was formed and now oversees all regional accrediting agencies and coordinates the work to advance self-regulation though accreditation. As of June 1997, it can be found on the World Wide Web at http://www.chea.org. As CHEA reviews all accreditation standards, it has a real opportunity to influence distance learning guidelines. In the meantime, the regional accrediting agencies are moving forward unilaterally.

Study and Methodology

Six regional accrediting agencies were contacted through a mail survey. Questions focused on the current policies and guidelines for distance learning, plans for the future revisions, and—as an example of applied policy—current guidelines for distance learning and libraries. The response rate was 100 percent. In addition to survey responses, current policies and accompanying memorandums addressing policy intent that were submitted by the agencies were also analyzed, and follow-up telephone interviews were conducted.

Findings: Stages of Policy Revision

Most agencies are vigorously studying how to address distance learning, but are in very different stages of considering revisions to current policies. For some of the accrediting commissions, separate policies are available for distance learning; many have no new policies. Many have adapted guidelines developed by one of two leading organizations, the American Council on Education (ACE) and the Western Cooperative for Educational Telecommunications of the Western Interstate Commission on Higher Education (WICHE). The ACE guidelines are titled *Guiding Principles for Distance Learning in a Learning Society* and take a strong learner-centered focus (Sullivan and Rocco, 1996). The Western Cooperative's guidelines (1996), *Principles of Good Practice for Electronically Offered Academic Degree and Certificate Programs,* are briefer but also offer good guidelines for practitioners. Both will be referred to throughout this chapter.

For some accrediting agencies, increased use of distance learning demands complex, separate standards. For others, it is a matter of principle to assure consistency across programs through integrated guidelines that do not reference where learning is delivered.

Survey Responses

Association for Community and Junior Colleges, Western Association of Schools and Colleges. This association has no explicit guidelines for distance learning. The current accreditation standards apply to all parts of the institution and include both traditional and nontraditional programs. The standards address competencies in student outcomes applicable to all educational activities "regardless of where or how presented or by whom taught" (Accrediting Commission, 1996, p. 3).

Further reference to distance learning embraces the guidelines provided through the American Council on Education's *Guiding Principles* (Sullivan and Rocco, 1996, p. 6).

Survey responses suggest that distance learning raises many questions for accreditors. The Western Commission's counterpart at the university level is identifying more specific criteria from which to evaluate distance learning, including delineation of how many miles away from the campus courses are offered, and general concurrence with the off-campus guidelines. It is likely that the introduction of new projects in the West, specifically the Western Governors University described in Chapter Seven, will result in more changes in regional policy.

Commission on Higher Education, Middle States Association of Colleges and Schools. Guidelines for distance learning programs were first presented March 1997. The authors conclude that "ultimately, the evaluation and accreditation of distance learning programs will rest on an institution's efforts to demonstrate that it accepts and complies with the Commission on Higher Education's standards for accreditation" (Commission on Higher Education, 1996, p. 1).

The commission introduced the requirement that institutions must explicitly state the rationale for entering into distance learning. The processes, policies, goals, and curricula of the distance learning programs must be clearly stated and must be consistent with those "established for other learning environments" (Commission on Higher Education, 1996, p. 2). All academic programs and support services must be appropriate for this new delivery system. Since many such programs incorporate technology-based programming developed outside the institution, the commission notes the importance of validating the academic credibility of such materials. The curriculum, too, must be reviewed for congruency with other curricula of the institution, allowing for ease of movement through all available programs.

Student outcomes will be measured as part of the commission's new guidelines, which require faculty and administrators to articulate clearly the benefits to students as these relate to "costs, learning effectiveness, ease of use, and access to the appropriate information and learning technologies" (Commission on Higher Education, 1996, p. 2). The standards also encourage collaborative group learning and consistent applications of technology for distance learning.

Middle States identifies distance learning and the use of distributed learning as catalysts for faculty innovation in helping learners achieve their educational goals. As the faculty role shifts to encompass that of course administrator or manager, the selection and training of faculty becomes critical to the success of the distance learning program. The commission emphasizes the need for substantive support to faculty to manage a distance learning course, including "access to computers, fax machines, and long distance telephone lines" (Commission on Higher Education, 1996, p. 4). Compensation models may need revision to respond to the changing demands on faculty time for development and course preparation. Central to the success of programs is the role of site administrators, distribution clerks, library resource personnel, and other support staff.

The Middle States guidelines address the importance of parity for distance learners in terms of educational outcomes, credit transferability, financial aid eligibility, and professional certification. Additional guidelines require that "administrators, managers, and coordinators possess not only technical proficiency in distance learning technology but a thorough understanding of how the distance learning activity is inextricably linked to the institutional mission and to the assessment of institutional effectiveness" (Commission on Higher Education, 1996, p. 8).

The emphasis on proper staffing is important to the success of such programs and a strong component of accreditation standards. Repeatedly, the commission stresses the importance of linking these courses and programs to institutional mission, including proper funding and facilities in light of the overall direction of the college. Commitment from the administration, faculty, and staff must be demonstrated to "ensure the continuity and integrity of the program" (Commission on Higher Education, 1996, p. 9).

Middle States takes its guidelines further than many in noting the importance of marketing the distance learning programs clearly, insisting on full disclosure of the requirements in all publications. Also discussed are decisions regarding copyright, fair use, and intellectual property. The Middle States guidelines are very sophisticated and offer an excellent model for other accrediting agencies struggling with standards for distance learning.

Commission on Higher Education, New England Association of Schools and Colleges. Although no specific policies for distance learning exist at this time, current standards have applicability, according to survey respondents. They observe that institutions whose policies, practices, or resources differ significantly from those described in the *Standards for Accreditation* must present evidence that these are appropriate to higher education, consistent with institutional mission and purposes, and effective in meeting the commission standards.

The commission noted that the proliferation of distance education programs as well as the commission's commitment to equity in decision making necessitates the development of a uniform set of principles for such evaluations. Respondents' comments parallel other agencies' observation that the time for the reformation of policy has clearly arrived.

Although there are no separate standards, the respondents noted that the visiting team of accreditors customarily includes evaluators with experience and expertise at institutions where distance learning is a major part of their activity. The commission is reviewing distance learning through continuing discussions and anticipates that this review will be ongoing. Issues to be addressed include the nature of faculty-student interaction, incentives for faculty, training and support, special facilities and equipment, methods for assessing quality, and effects on governance, advising, and the curriculum (Commission on Higher Education, New England Association of Schools and Colleges, memorandum dated June 5, 1996, p. 6).

North Central Association of Colleges and Schools, Commission on Institutions of Higher Education. North Central endorses the WICHE Principles, and plans to integrate these guidelines into their next handbook. While they have no official statement on distance learning other than this endorsement, the agency uses existing guidelines on institutional change in looking at significant distance learning requests. (See North Central Association of Colleges and Schools, 1992, 1994, 1995.)

The guidelines include assurances of strong planning and accountability for new programs. These criteria may be difficult to meet for many distance learning programs. Not all campus-based programs will withstand the scrutiny required by the guidelines either. It is important to recognize that distance learners deserve strong guidelines to assure a quality education; the guidelines must not, however, be more limiting or more stringent than those applied at other programs.

North Central is currently considering the possibility of developing its own statement about the commission's expectations for distance learning instead of relying solely on the WICHE guidelines.

Northwest Association of Schools and Colleges, Commission on Colleges. The Northwest Association is exploring ways to address distance learning, and has adapted the WICHE guidelines (Northwest Association of Schools and Colleges, 1996). The focus of current standards is on compatibility of policies, methods, and delivery systems with the institutional goals and mission—but the Northwest Association plans to examine all education as part of the greater institutional effort. The determining factor in quality of distance learning, it notes, will be the institution's intent. As guidelines are reviewed, one commission member stressed that everyone has a stake in positive outcomes.

Southern Association of Colleges and Schools, Commission on Colleges. The Southern Association has clearly defined guidelines for distance learning, stating "Institutions offering courses for credit through distance learning activities *must* meet all criteria related to faculty. Whether through direct contact or other appropriate means, institutions offering distance learning programs must provide students with structured access to and interaction with full-time faculty members" (Southern Association of Colleges and Schools, 1992, p. 49).

The Southern Association's guidelines specifically address evaluation of distance learning programs, requiring the distance learning evaluator to carefully review the institution's organizational chart and administrative structure to ensure accountability for distance learning activities. This is an important criterion not mentioned by many accreditors. It implies that the placement of distance learning within the organizational setting may speak loudly for the institution's commitment to the courses or programs.

Specific guidelines require the distance learning evaluator to assure that the visiting accreditation team address all relevant courses and programs offered away from the campus. As with other accrediting agencies, the link to the college's mission is critical. Evaluators must ask whether distance learning is part of the broader institutional plan and then delve into faculty, staffing, and other related issues.

One of the greatest challenges for distance learning is the research base, often not sufficient to convince faculty and administrators to offer technology-based courses away from campus. The Southern Association requires research and evaluation as part of distance learning programs. The standards then require full justification of choices, locations, planning, curriculum development, and a variety of process-related issues.

The selection and qualification of the faculty is noted in the separate distance learning standards. These standards are designed to ensure that the academic qualifications of distance teaching faculty are the same as on-campus faculty, and also address the level of experience of faculty working in this type of distance learning activity.

In cases where the institution participates in a consortium or contractual relationship with an outside party, the Southern Association includes evaluation criteria for those partnerships. These criteria ask whether or not the arrangements have been documented, and if student services are guaranteed.

Educational support services are strongly emphasized. The criteria address the need to target student development activities specifically to students involved in distance learning, and the need to demonstrate that the availability of these services is well communicated to distance learners. The standards also mandate assessment of administrative and fiscal commitment. Finally, in reviewing a college's self-study process, the Southern Association requires detailed inclusion of distance learning program reviews. Colleges and universities must document how such programs were assessed in the self-study and by whom. For new programs, the Southern Association also has separate, detailed *Guidelines for Planning Distance Learning Activities*.

Principles of Good Practice for Electronically Delivered Academic Degree and Certificate Programs. The *Principles*, developed by the Western Cooperative for Educational Telecommunications of the Western Cooperative for Higher Education (WICHE), were a response to higher education's quickened rate of adding programs offered through distance learning. They are not meant to serve as a substitute for the standards for accreditation of agencies, which apply to all educational activities offered "in the name of the institution, regardless of where or how presented, or by whom taught" (Western Cooperative for Educational Telecommunications, 1996, p. 1). They do, however, serve as a good framework for institutions developing and evaluating distance learning programs.

The *WICHE Principles* include sections on curriculum and instruction that outline programs of study to include outcomes, coherency, completion, alternate delivery times, interaction, and faculty oversight. Within the institutional context and commitment, the *Principles* note the importance of fitting distance learning programs into the context of institutional role and mission. They further emphasize the need for faculty support and training, support resources, timely and adequate student support services, marketing efforts, and assessment.

The *Principles* reinforce the need for the institutions to commit the support of faculty, finances, and technical resources. While many institutions may introduce programs without a commitment to continuation, the WICHE standards encourage support for "continuation of the program for a period sufficient to enable students to complete a degree/certificate" (Western Cooperative for Educational Telecommunications, 1996, p. 3). To assure quality within the program, guidelines encourage evaluation and assessment of student learning outcomes, student retention, and student and faculty satisfaction. Students should have access to this evaluation data, and assessment of student achievement should be provided at both the course and program level.

Guiding Principles for Distance Learning in a Learning Society. In May 1996, the American Council on Education (ACE) introduced this document as an outgrowth of a concern for quality education and training opportunities for adults. The Center for Adult Learning and Educational Credentials formed a broad-based task force to develop the principles. Their partner in this effort was the Alliance: An Association for Alternative Degree Programs for Adults, of which approximately 125 members are colleges and universities.

The Preface to the *Guidelines* notes that "the task force had two key insights. The first was that the digital revolution has altered previous limitations of time and space in a profound way. In this era, when time and space have only relative existences, we lead new lives—ones in which we are no longer children of time or space, to paraphrase Emerson. . . . [The second insight was] that learning permeates many sectors of society, therefore principles of good practice must not be applicable only to institutions of higher education" (Sullivan and Rocco, 1996, pp. 1–2). This focus is central to the development of these guidelines, emphasizing the involvement of all those in the learning enterprise, including individual learners, institutions, corporations, labor unions, associations, and government agencies.

Authors of the *Guidelines* identified four key issues—the impact of technology advances, quality assurance, student-centered programs, and core values in a learning society. The development of values moves these guidelines away from a strict focus on distance learning, placing distance learning within the larger institutional context. Specifically, it is emphasized that the *Guidelines* do not constitute a "how to" list, but rather a "statement designed to address the qualities that should characterize the learning society in years ahead" (Sullivan and Rocco, 1996, p. 2).

One perspective that sets this document apart from the *WICHE Principles* is the emphasis on core values. For example, one core value states "Learning is a lifelong process, important to successful participation in the social, cultural, civic, and economic life of a democratic society" (Sullivan and Rocco, 1996, p. 3).

Central areas of concern defined and described in the *ACE Guidelines* include the context for learning, support for learners, organizational commitment, outcomes assessment, and the planning and infrastructure needed to support distance learning programs.

Achieving Parity in Distributed Learning

A fundamental conflict in devising standards for distance learning is whether distance learning programs should even have separate guidelines. One accrediting agency was adamant when interviewed that the problem with the ACE recommendations was the implication that distance learning needs its own guidelines. Other agencies were equally committed to the bifurcation of policies and standards, stating that without separate regulations distance learning will become substandard compared to on-campus programs.

Eventually, the lines must disappear between on-campus and distance learning. The requisites for the latter are clearly more rigid, implying that if a course is not taken on a college campus it will be inferior. But the opposite may also be true. If the accrediting agencies are concerned about support services, academic integrity, and other areas such as making sure registration is learner-centered, why then should they not evaluate traditional programs with equal rigor?

Regional-State Tensions

States have traditionally managed to oversee distributed learning through exist-ing organizations such as state regents or similar bodies headed up by a for-mal governance structure. When regional accrediting agencies are at odds with these structures, interesting tensions can develop—with the local college caught in the middle. Which master should the community college obey?

Too often states become their own bureaucratic stumbling blocks. Faculty-driven groups may be hesitant about introducing new (possibly threatening) technologies for education, and states respond by writing very conservative policies. But these policies are mute when other institutions beam their signals over state lines into the homes of all learners.

Ultimately, the choice between state and regional regulations must be guided by the educational needs of the learner. If institutions truly believe that they are offering quality programs through distance learning, they will rise to the occasion in ways that meet the needs of all their various masters. As the technologies grow at an increasing rate, all policymakers must accept that try-ing to force new learning paradigms into old policy frameworks is deadly for progress.

Unresolved Issues

Our system of accreditation has served as an important vehicle for quality assurance in higher education. Primary responsibility for quality assurance is a function of multiple levels of accountability that include the institution, the state, the regional accrediting agency, and specialized accrediting agencies. Dis-tributed learning is a force that requires a fundamental reexamination of the policies and procedures that define the business of higher education. It is important that community colleges be aware both of the issues involved and of the roles played by those responsible for quality assurance.

Important academic issues include the academic calendar, access and admissions, curriculum, evaluation of teachers and programs, mission com-pliance, and articulation. Fiscal policies must address tuition and fees, costs and cost sharing, revenue sharing, and financial commitment. Service issues include the relationship between community college and four-year-plus pro-grams, interstate agreements, and the viability of geographic service areas. Labor management issues include class size, compensation, copyright and intellectual property rights, incentives and development, workload, and train-ing. Support service issues include advising, counseling, libraries, marketing, and access to course resources. Finally, organizational and governance issues include the role of state, institutional, and consortial boards, staffing, and orga-nizational structure for distance learning.

Community colleges offering distance programs are at the center of a fluid policy development environment. Guidelines are often in conflict, and as mul-tistate consortia grow, there will be new organizations seeking accreditation across state lines and even across regions. To date, the commissions determining accreditation criteria have not reached consensus on how to handle those challenges.

Much progress has been made in the last five years with respect to assuring quality programs through distance learning. Biases against distance programs are still very much in evidence, and skeptics abound. Nonetheless, distance learning technologies are growing at a rate that outpaces our ability to develop sufficient guidelines. The challenges are enormous, and very real—so, too, are the opportunities.

References

Accrediting Commission for Community and Junior Colleges. *Draft Standards of Accreditation.* Aptos, Calif.: Western Association of Schools and Colleges, May 1996.

Chaloux, B. *The Project on Assessing Long Distance Learning Via Telecommunications: Project ALLTEL.* Denver, Colo.: Council on Postsecondary Accreditation and State Higher Education Executive Officers Association, 1985.

Commission on Higher Education, Middle States Association of Colleges and Schools. *Draft Distance Learning Policy Statement.* Philadelphia: Middle States Association of Colleges and Schools, Sept. 1996.

North Central Association of Colleges and Schools, Commission on Institutions of Higher Education. *Adopted Revisions of the General Institutional Requirements, the Criteria for Accreditation, and the Candidacy Program.* Chicago: North Central Association of Colleges and Schools, Commission on Institutions of Higher Education, 1992.

North Central Association of Colleges and Schools, Commission on Institutions of Higher Education. *Handbook of Accreditation 1994–1996.* Chicago: North Central Association of Colleges and Schools, Commission on Institutions of Higher Education, 1994.

North Central Association of Colleges and Schools, Commission on Institutions of Higher Education. *Accreditation of Higher Education Institutions: An Overview.* Chicago: North Central Association of Colleges and Schools, Commission on Institutions of Higher Education, 1995.

Northwest Association of Schools and Colleges. *Standard Two—Educational Program and Its Effectiveness.* Seattle: Northwest Association of Schools and Colleges, 1996.

Southern Association of Colleges and Schools, Commission on Colleges. *Evaluation Considerations for Distance Learning.* Decatur, Ga: Southern Association of Colleges and Schools, Commission on Colleges, 1992.

Sullivan, E., and Rocco, T. *Guiding Principles for Distance Learning in a Learning Society.* Washington, D.C.: American Council on Education, 1996.

Western Cooperative for Educational Telecommunications. *Principles of Good Practice for Electronically Offered Academic Degree and Certificate Programs.* Boulder, Colo.: Western Interstate Commission for Higher Education, 1996.

BARBARA GELLMAN-DANLEY is vice president for educational technology at Monroe Community College. She has over twenty years' experience in distance learning administration and consults extensively on policy development.

As the communication technologies of today challenge the traditional concept of ownership, community colleges must address copyright and intellectual property issues.

Ownership and Access: Copyright and Intellectual Property in the On-Line Environment

Marina Stock McIsaac, Jeremy Rowe

The new semester has begun at City Community College. You have been preparing materials for a new course, Introduction to Multimedia, to be offered on the World Wide Web. After hours of searching for high-quality materials to support your course, you have finally located just what you need. You tell a colleague, "I'm really excited about what I've found for the students. We've got video clips from Disney, and I'm going to use Macromedia Director. There are some great journal articles I've found on the Web and I'm putting those in my on-line bibliography. I even found a good-looking Web site out there that I can use by copying the html. This is really going to be fun!"

You assemble your class resources and prepare handouts so your students can download the program and video clips directly to their desktops. By the end of the first few weeks of classes, students have found National Geographic and PBS clips to add to the course resources and the class seems to be a great success. As you return to your office at City Community College, your secretary hands you a registered letter. A law firm representing Disney productions is citing you for violation of copyright. What do you do?

This scenario may become a more frequent occurrence as teachers across the country are encouraged to put their class materials on the Internet or World Wide Web. As teachers begin to enhance their courses with visuals, video clips, and sound bites, the issue of what material can be used becomes a vital concern.

Why Worry About Copyright?

The rapid expansion of communication technologies has been accompanied by a growing interest in the issues of copyright and intellectual property rights. Electronic storage and transfer of text and images has made cutting and pasting a way of life. With words and pictures so easily available, concerns about the protection of the intellectual property of the creators of written and graphic materials are increasing.

The recent growth of the Internet has exacerbated these concerns. Viewers can easily capture and modify articles, photographs, video clips, and graphics. Indeed, in many cases Internet users believe that if an article or picture is on the Net, it is free for the taking. The "access equals permission to use" philosophy has been deeply disturbing to those concerned with copyright and enforcement of intellectual property rights and has complicated negotiations for guidelines to allow educational fair use without obtaining permission. These issues have widespread implications for distance educators.

Educators must demand that effective policies be developed in the areas of copyright, fair use, duplication, and revenue generation for print and non-print educational materials. These policies must address the needs of both the copyright holder and the end user. As educators begin to develop and market their own programs and assume the role of copyright owner, they often begin to view the issues of control and access differently. Copyright and intellectual property issues will be key to the success of all technology-based educational efforts. All groups have a stake in how these important policy issues are addressed.

Legal and Licensing Issues

From a copyright or intellectual property perspective, faculty-produced materials for distance learning differ significantly from materials used in the classroom. Copyright guidelines established for educational fair use specify face-to-face instruction and interpretations vary with regard to their application to materials distributed to students at remote sites over video or computer networks. Much of the focus of this debate relates to whether or not remote instructional sites qualify as face-to-face instruction. Typically educators favor the inclusion of such sites, while producers, distributors, and publishers do not. For example, the recently negotiated "Fair Use Guidelines for Educational Multi-Media" limit the use of multimedia materials to:

- Remote real-time instruction to students enrolled in curriculum-based courses (that is, no recorded or rebroadcast courses)
- Transmissions over a network in a manner that prevents making copies of copyrighted materials

The limitations of real-time instruction and security requirements serve as formidable barriers to many distance education applications. (For more information on the guidelines, see the following World Wide Web site: http://www.lib.berkeley.edu/MRC/kastenmeier.html.)

Legislation, case law, and institutional policies—already difficult to apply to copyright issues in contained classrooms—fail to address the power of the video and computer networks used in distance education today. Furthermore, policies that inadequately address infringement and permission as applied to slides copied from reference books and use of off-air or recorded videotape completely fail to deal with issues of licensing, permissions for broadcast, or computer distribution. Faculty and students can copy, modify, and distribute materials without understanding the implications or potential institutional ramifications of copyright and intellectual property rights. From an administrative perspective, concerns can be categorized into issues related to:

- Faculty-produced material that incorporates elements whose copyright is controlled by others, or faculty use of commercial products
- Student-produced material and the releases or permissions that should be obtained to use student materials in distance education contexts
- Team-produced material and the issues of ownership surrounding crediting and assignment of ownership and the implications associated with future use of materials produced by production teams involving faculty, students, instructional designers, and production staff

Course Materials on the Internet. The Internet raises a number of issues that further complicate the educational use of copyrighted materials. From its origins in the ARPANET and BITNET, the Internet developed in an atmosphere of cooperation and collaboration. In the early days, commercial products were few and information being transmitted was primarily text. The "culture of sharing" that evolved from these early days has clashed with the concept of ownership as defined by the protections and rights outlined in copyright and intellectual property law. The economic potential of electronic versions of traditional media such as books, photographs, graphics, and video has renewed commercial interests relative to licensing and commercialization.

During this same period, distance education evolved from broadcast to satellite, microwave, and cable distribution for video materials. Now computers and network capabilities make it possible for educators to reach vast new student populations. Production capabilities available to the average user permit scanning and video capture, and the Internet provides convenient access to millions of text, graphic, and video resources. The ability of faculty, staff, and students to acquire, modify, and create materials using technology-based resources reflects technological advances unimaginable to the Congress drafting the 1978 copyright law.

Electronic Publication Rights. Electronic publication rights provide another area that has increased in complexity due to the increasing commercialization of the Internet. Few community college faculty members are aware of the considerations associated with the assignment or licensing of their intellectual property when negotiating publishing contracts. Some of these considerations include rights to derivative works, display, performance, and distribution in electronic as well as print media.

Many contracts assign copyright to the publisher and include broad print and electronic rights. Unless specified in the contract, faculty who sign away the copyright for their work may be required to obtain permission and pay copyright fees to the publisher to duplicate and use their own work. Electronic distribution may also address any revenue derived from licensed duplication through services such as Uncover, which provides access to materials by charging service and copyright fees. The copyright fees range from a few dollars to almost $100 with a significant portion of the copyright fee going to the copyright holder.

The process of obtaining print or electronic rights to use copyrighted materials is time consuming, and provides no guarantees that the copyright holder will permit use of the material. In addition, if permission is granted, cost and guidelines for use vary dramatically. Important considerations in requesting permission for print material include the number of copies, proportion of the work to be duplicated, and how competitive the reproduction is with sales of the text or reprint. Electronic rights are even more difficult to assess when deciding whether to grant permission and what fees to charge. Some copyright holders may be flexible and permit electronic use, but may limit access by requiring passwords. Others may charge exorbitant fees. Many will not permit any electronic use at all.

Transmission over video or computer networks—common for distance education courses—involves electronic rights when printed material is captured by the video camera and scanned into a document or used as a graphic. These conversions of media are derivative works and even relatively liberal interpretations of the guidelines indicate that permission of the copyright holder is needed if such materials are distributed over networks.

A great fear among producers is losing control of material that is available electronically. Duplication is extremely easy and the result of a single open posting can significantly affect the market for the material in print. Potential loss of revenue coupled with the complexity and current unreliability of billing for individual use considerably complicates the process of obtaining permissions for electronic use of copyrighted material. Faculty wishing to post their articles on the Internet should check the contract and publication agreements to determine if they have retained the right to do so. For future publications, authors should consider potential use of their materials, retaining the rights necessary to use their work.

Faculty members typically acquire materials to support their teaching from a variety of sources, often using broadcast materials, videotape, films, slides, CD-ROM software, and Internet materials. The penalties associated with violation of copyright can be severe. Fair use guidelines represent an attempt to accommodate the needs of traditional classroom applications.

Fair Use

Initial efforts to provide flexibility and permit justification for the educational use of copyrighted materials in a limited context without the need to obtain permission resulted in the Agreement on Guidelines for Classroom Copying in Not-For-Profit Educational Institutions (1976). The guidelines (in section 107 of H.R. 2223) state the minimum standards allowable for educational uses of copyrighted material. These include "criticism, comment, news reporting, teaching (including multiple copies for classroom use), scholarship, or research" (p. 65). The guidelines then stipulate four factors that are considered when determining fair use.

• The purpose and character of the use
• The nature of the copyrighted work
• The amount and substantiality of the portion used in relation to the whole work
• The effect on the potential market for or value of the copyrighted work

Although the use of copyrighted material without permission is an infringement, the fair use guidelines provide a framework for the justification to waive liability if all four of the criteria have been met.

The perspective of what is acceptable and what is infringement forms a continuum from the view of the user (who is interested in economical access) to the publisher, producer, or copyright holder (who are all interested in protecting rights to a work). Even an author who intends to freely distribute a work is usually interested in receiving due credit if the work is distributed or reproduced. Interestingly, the guidelines readily acknowledge that technological developments may affect the interpretation of fair use in the future.

Because the fair use guidelines are broad and open to varying interpretation by faculty, librarians, media professionals, and administrators, the courts and various agencies have provided additional direction in refining the concept of fair use. The National Commission on New Technological Uses of Copyrighted Works addressed fair use in the CONTU report (Committee on the Judiciary, 1978). In addition, the Conference on Fair Use also issued some draft guidelines, available on-line at http://www.utsystem.edu/ogc/intellectualproperty/confu.htm. Although these guidelines have finally evolved to a point of effectively addressing print duplication, they are still working on issues such as library reserve and interlibrary loan. Unfortunately, the evolution of policy falls far behind the needs of distance educators, computer networks, Internet developers, or the myriad of other people using technology in education today. The laws and policies cannot develop quickly enough to guide the application of technology, which today changes exponentially.

The Kastenmeier Guidelines represented an initial attempt to address off-air recording of broadcast video materials by nonprofit educational institutions (Congressional Record, 1984). The guidelines are vague in their application to cable and satellite distribution and do not permit editing or rebroadcast over educational television systems unless it is to dedicated classrooms—see Section 110(2). These omissions again limit the usefulness of the guidelines for many video applications in distance education.

The tremendous growth of the Internet and WWW together with the changing role of higher education from a contained classroom model to a distributed media model has profound implications for fair use. Technologies such as video (via satellite and cable) and the WWW drastically change the ground rules for using educational materials that are not self-produced.

In 1993, the Consortium of College and University Media Centers (CCUMC) began to assemble interested parties to establish guidelines for multimedia. The CCUMC Fair Access Working Committee brought together representatives from the education, software, publishing, broadcast music, motion picture, and video industries to begin discussions designed to establish guidelines for the educational use of copyrighted materials in distance education (Consortium of College and University Media Centers, 1995).

From the educator's perspective, the intent was to broaden access to materials without the need to spend time locating and obtaining permission from the copyright holders. Because the interests of copyright holders lie in protecting the market for their materials, they have acknowledged that their interests might be served by slightly broader interpretations of nonprofit educational use rather than narrow restrictions that could be costly and difficult to enforce.

After significant negotiations but well before closure, a series of draft guidelines were drawn up and used as the basis for discussion at a teleconference, primarily for educators (Consortium of College and University Media Centers, 1995). The action of the CCUMC workgroup was slowed by the concerns of network distribution of copyrighted materials by educational users (Jacobson, 1995).

Thought not universally endorsed, the guidelines have been supported by organizations such as the Instructional Telecommunications Council and the American Association of Community Colleges. These guidelines are initial attempts to address a number of critical issues including what materials can be used, time limits, acceptable portions, copies, and use over distance learning systems (Dalziel, 1997). However, many issues remain unresolved for use in distance education, including student limits at remote sites and the requirement that delivery technology prevent copying.

Even the more liberal distance learning fair use guidelines proposed in the CONTU discussions limit fair use to nonprofit educational activities "transmitted over a secure system with limited access" for single, one-time use. Other factors that limit potential distance education use include references to "classrooms or other places normally devoted to instruction" that are "directly related and of material assistance to the teaching content." In addition, any copies retained for student use may not be reproduced and must be erased not more than fifteen days after transmission. For computer-based material, the guidelines remove the restriction of a classroom or instructional space, but do not allow copying by individual students. These guidelines are available on-line at http://www.utsystem.edu/ogc/intellectualproperty/distguid.htm.

Two key factors influence the importance of the Internet and its impact on educational administrators. The first is the change from paper copies handed out in the traditional, self-contained educational classroom that is assumed in copyright guidelines to increasingly distributed, "published" documents available via network to students and the community. Like other extended educational applications, the potential size of the audience and the noneducational nature of the transmission media shift Internet applications toward the commercial end of the continuum in the eye of the public and policymakers.

The second factor is the growing awareness of materials available on the Internet. The public perceives the Internet as a tool of commerce. The economic potential of using the network is driving policy discussions relative to licensing, and has greatly restricted more liberal copyright use permits. Prime evidence is the current trend to tighten restrictions for educational use and the strong movement to empower the copyright holder as evident in the current National Information Infrastructure white paper (Lehman, 1995).

Recent efforts to revise copyright law have involved recommendations that significantly shift the balance of fair use by strengthening the rights of the copyright holder and limiting the ability to use materials without obtaining permission. As the Internet increasingly reaches a broad and affluent marketplace, information providers such as publishers and distributors will likely increase efforts to reach much broader markets than they previously targeted. Thus efforts to market more broadly appear to significantly affect the impact of the specific use on potential marketability, a key fair use criterion.

Duplication Infringements

The rapid expansion of communication technologies like the World Wide Web has challenged the concept of fair use, and teachers are venturing into uncharted waters. Materials that they once would have duplicated for single-classroom use are now being distributed across networks and are suddenly available to a much larger audience.

Policies to regulate duplication are not able to keep up with the development of reproduction technologies. Browsers and scanners have changed the way in which documents and images are used and exchanged. What once took hours now can be done in minutes. Images and text can be used, transformed, and reused in a variety of formats. Files can be easily captured, stored, and reused—often without an acknowledgment for their creator. Images can be manipulated and revised at will. All these duplication infringements occur in the absence of firm policies to deter the person doing the duplicating. Indeed, many people are unaware that they are violating the intellectual property rights of others when they borrow an image from the Web or scan an article to send to their class.

Perhaps the most visible example of duplication infringement can be found on the thousands of home pages springing up on the Web. The broad range of technologies that are suddenly available, and the ease of placing text, video, and graphics on a home page, exacerbates the problem. Without a clear policy outlining what is and what is not acceptable in terms of duplicating, teachers will continue to use what is available to them. As technologies allow duplication to become easier and faster, problems for educators, publishers, and producers of original material will continue to grow.

Revenue Generation and Faculty Ownership

Another issue that must be addressed is ownership of materials. Although in business materials produced by employees are considered to be the property of the employer as works-for-hire, academia has not had a similar tradition. Books and articles written by faculty members at community colleges and universities have been considered the intellectual property of the faculty member. Recently, as teams of teachers and production staff have developed software or courseware together, the issue of ownership has become increasingly complex. Educational institutions, seeing that the development of multimedia materials has become lucrative, are becoming interested in their fair share of the revenue.

The development of Internet courses raises questions concerning who owns the course, the faculty or the institution. Issues surrounding production incentives such as overload pay, release time, and institutional rewards are convincing administrators that materials developed using college resources rightfully belong to the college. When faculty work results in money being returned to the college, where should those funds go? Should they be returned to a local account, to the faculty member, or to general institutional overhead? Policies that clearly outline ownership are common in regard to patents in many research universities. However, few community colleges address the issues of ownership of courses and curriculum materials in their faculty contracts or policies. Therefore, when questions of control or revenue distribution arise, faculty and administrators must react with little guidance or direction, usually only after the issue has become a concern to one or both parties.

Student-produced materials pose an additional problem. If a student produces a product for class, who owns the product? If the student is hired to produce a product (on a grant, for example), who owns the product? What is the difference between work for hire and contracting services in terms of intellectual property rights? Unlike the private sector, academia has traditionally allowed creators to retain ownership. Colleges must address troubling issues such as ownership and control of instructional materials, and policies must protect both the individual and the institution.

Conclusion

The issues surrounding copyright and intellectual property are very complex, and operate in an ever-changing environment. To avoid finding themselves in the position of responding to a cease-and-desist letter from a publisher as described in the opening of this chapter, teachers and administrators need to be aware of copyright and ownership concerns and work to develop and implement appropriate policies. Critical decisions must be made based on interpretations of general policies rather than on firm guidelines. One way to begin to understand and address the issues of copyright and intellectual property in education is as a continuum from low to high levels of risk. Policy and guidelines can be used to define the continuum in general terms. Informed administrators and counsel must then determine a point or range that represents an appropriate risk level. Finally, institutional policies and procedures must be developed to support that position. Some of the key elements appropriate to address in institutional policies include:

- Efforts to educate and increase awareness about copyright and intellectual property issues and relevant institutional policies
- Ways to access information and assistance in obtaining licensing, clearances, and answers to copyright and intellectual property questions
- Resources available to provide access to licensed originally produced materials
- Criteria for establishing ownership and procedures for using materials produced by faculty and students at the institution (print, multimedia, and intellectual property in addition to patents)
- Consequences for violation of institutional policies, and procedures for appeal from those consequences

Comprehensive institutional policies will provide some protection to the institution while lending credibility to educators and librarians in their efforts to shape national and international policies and laws that support educational use and increase access to our communities.

Publishers, producers, and other creators of materials have been the driving force behind recent efforts to address these issues. Studies such as the National Information Infrastructure green and white papers on copyright have had little initial input from libraries and educators. As a result, they generally recommend strengthening the position of the copyright holder while restricting public access and educational use without proper licensing. An intense effort by educational and library organizations slowed this process down and returned educational use and public access to the national debate.

This new role of advocacy will grow in importance as the use of technology in education and libraries provides increasing access by remote users. Critical to this process are the continuation of cooperative discussions between the various interests such as the Consortium of College and University Media Centers and their work with publishers and media producers. Discussions such as these should be encouraged to ensure the development of effective licensing models and procedures designed to address the needs of both users and copyright holders.

Swifter procedures for obtaining copyright permission must be devised. In this period of change when institutions of higher education are resizing, reengineering, and reinventing themselves, the technological revolution offers a variety of solutions to problems of classroom space, course delivery, and differentiated staffing.

Telecommunications licensing and copyright issues are two areas in which federal legislation must move ahead to keep pace with technology, if educators are to truly benefit from the technological revolution. Higher education must be aggressive in helping to formulate telecommunication and copyright policy at the national level. Without the input of educators, the telecommunication industry will formulate policies that may not serve the interests of education. It is essential that the higher education community learn how to compete in this new electronic marketplace and extend the reach of campuses into the home and workplace.

References

Agreement on Guidelines for Classroom Copying in Not-For-Profit Educational Institutions. Copyright Law Revision of 1976, H.R. Rep. No. 94–1476, 94th Cong., 2d sess. 68. Washington, D.C.: U.S. Government Printing Office, 1976, pp. 68–70.

Committee on the Judiciary. Final Report of the National Commission on New Technological Uses of Copyrighted Works. Washington, D.C.: U.S. Government Printing Office, 1978.

Congressional Record 1984, 98th Cong., 2d sess., vol. 130, pt. 17: 24048–24049. Off Air Recording Guidelines Named for Congressman Robert Kastenmeier, Chairman of the House Subcommittee on Courts, Civil Liberties and Administration of Justice.

Consortium of College and University Media Centers. Multimedia Fair Use Guidelines: The Educational Gateway to the Information Age. PBS Adult Learning Satellite Services teleconference materials, Sept. 21, 1995.

Dalziel, C. "AACC and ITC Endorse Fair Use Guidelines for Educational Multimedia." ITC News, 1997, 9 (6), 1–2.

Jacobson, R. L. "Publishers' Group Balks at Key Provision in Proposed Guidelines on "Fair Use." Chronicle of Higher Education, 1995, 42 (17), A23.

Lehman, B. A. Intellectual Property and the National Information Infrastructure: Report of the Working Group on Intellectual Property Rights. Information Infrastructure Task Force. Washington, D.C.: U.S. Government Printing Office, 1995.

MARINA STOCK MCISAAC is professor of educational media and computers at Arizona State University. She has been a Fulbright Senior Scholar/Researcher working in distance education in Turkey, Germany, and Italy and has published more than sixty articles and book chapters.

JEREMY ROWE is currently head of media development for information technology at Arizona State University. He has been involved in instructional design and media management for seventeen years at the community college and university levels.

This chapter analyzes the literature related to distance education in the community college environment, and looks ahead to new areas of inquiry.

Distance Education and the Community College: From Convention to Vision

Connie L. Dillon, Rosa Cintrón

As distance education plays an increasingly dominant role in community college education, it stands to alter the function of the community college at a time when the community college is poised to challenge traditional conceptions of higher education. Brey (1991) documents significant increases in the number of community colleges that are using and planning to use distance education. These figures surpass both the actual and anticipated use of distance education in other sectors of higher education. Two-year colleges make up the largest sector of higher education, in both numbers of institutions and enrollments. The forces predicted to serve as catalysts for change in higher education—increasing diversity in student population, new partnerships with business, and competition from commercial providers—have a strong influence on the community college (Rossman, 1992). Community colleges are often the first to venture beyond predictable and comfortable borders in higher education, seeking to fulfill their open-door mission and tradition of community service.

This volume has made clear that until now, the response to the innovation of distance education has been dominated by questions of effectiveness. Considerable further research is needed to help us better understand how to use telecommunications effectively in education. But technological change may force us to rethink the very meaning of effectiveness in education—so some new questions are in order.

Our exploration of the current literature was organized into three thematic areas identified as important by community college leaders (Morrison, 1995):

learners and learning, teachers and teaching, and mission and boundaries. For each theme we addressed old questions that have been answered and emerging questions that must be answered as we move into the next millennium.

Learners and Learning

Whenever a new instructional technology is developed, the first question we seek to answer is whether the new technology is as good as what we used in the past. In the field of distance learning, effectiveness has been defined in terms of learning, persistence, and attitudes, but the most prevalent questions are those related to learning.

Delivery system does not appear to influence learning, whether comparing conventional instruction with television instruction (Chu and Schramm, 1975), with computer instruction (Kulik and Kulik, 1980, 1986), with multimedia instruction (Fletcher, 1990; McNeil and Nelson, 1991), or with distance instruction (Whittington, 1988; Moore and Thompson, 1990). When the comparative studies focus explicitly on community colleges, the findings are similar (MacBrayne, 1995; Blanchard, 1989; Nixon, 1992).

However, it can be argued that the premise that conventional education is the appropriate standard of excellence for twenty-first-century education is flawed. Conventional instruction may not accommodate individual learner needs (Berman, Wyman, and Kunz, 1972); it fails to adjust for differences among learners in terms of time required to master a learning task. It also binds students and teachers to a common time and place, and it provides limited access to the "world brain" (Rossman, 1992).

The Medium-Method Dilemma. Although we may clearly conclude from the research that any delivery system can be used to teach any content, there is also evidence that different instructional strategies are more effective for different learning tasks. For instance, some research indicates that lecture strategies may be a better choice for information learning than for problem solving (Weston and Cranton, 1986). For information learning, a videotape presentation has certain advantages over a face-to-face presentation: the simultaneous presentation of voice, pictures, and words (Nugent, 1982); the opportunity to review the material; the availability of a variety of cuing strategies to direct attention (Schramm, 1977); and the ease of placing new concepts (Tennyson, 1996). Audio conferencing technologies may be appropriate for tasks that require group discussion or case study strategies (Gilcher and Johnstone, 1989). The concreteness of a video conference may be the preferred choice for tasks that require motion (Schramm, 1977). Likewise, conferencing systems may be preferable to taped systems when the task requires immediate feedback (Moore and Kearsley, 1996) or learner involvement in instructional decisions. Therefore our new questions must help us understand the relationship between learning tasks, instructional strategies, and delivery system attributes.

Individualized Learning and Within-Group Differences. One of the promises of distance education is as a vehicle for responding to the increasing diversity in higher education, whether diversity of culture, gender, age, experience, or educational needs (Jonsen and Johnstone, 1991; Duning, Van Kekerix, and Zaborowski, 1993). Research shows that certain learner characteristics may interact with delivery systems to affect performance. For example, the need for external motivation may be more important for low-motivated students in individualized distance education systems than for low-motivated learners in interactive systems (Bruning, Landis, Hoffman, and Grosskopf, 1993; Cookson, 1989). High aptitude and confidence in the ability to learn content also may interact with delivery system to affect performance (Bruning, Landis, Hoffman, and Grosskopf, 1993). Dille and Mezak (1991) found evidence that students who place the responsibility for their performance upon themselves may perform better in a more independent environment than students who place the responsibility for their performance on external factors. Gibson (1996) describes a dynamic learner whose motivation, confidence, and context change throughout the distance learning experience.

Dropout: Is Distance Education a Solution or Part of the Problem? Community college students typically spend little time in social or volunteer activities on campus, since they face an array of competing responsibilities to family and work. This lack of involvement has helped explain the retention problems of two-year colleges. More recent studies indicate that for those students who were successful in completing an associate degree, contact with faculty members was an important ingredient in their success (Tinto, 1993).

There is also evidence that persistence in distance education is not a function of delivery system but rather a function of the quality of interaction with teachers and peers (Holmberg, 1985; Powell, Conway, and Ross, 1990; Garrison, 1990; Holt, Petzall, and Viljoen, 1990). By increasing the amount and quality of student and teacher contact, distance education could be one of the most powerful tools in solving our dropout problem. Distributed learning can enrich, expand, and even transform the human connections available to community college students (Reudenstine, 1997). Thus our research questions need to emphasize not the *distance* in distance education but the *connections* made possible by distance technologies.

Democratization and Opportunity: Reality or Facade? Another common body of research is designed to answer questions about who participates in distance education. That research shows in general that distance education serves a greater proportion of women than men, a greater proportion of Caucasians than minorities (Brey and Grigsby, 1984; Pugliese, 1994; Dillon, 1997), and upper-income populations at greater rates than lower-income populations (Brock, 1990; Dede, 1994).

The promise of distance education is increased access. Proponents of distance education have cited its potential to reach the disabled, the homebound, the isolated, and the economically and educationally disadvantaged (Berman, Wyman, and Kunz, 1972; Jonsen and Johnstone, 1991). But data suggest that the promise of increased accessibility is not being realized. Duning, Van Kekerix, and Zaborowski (1993) state that traditional adult education programs do not serve minority and economically disadvantaged populations very well, suggesting that the costs and knowledge required to use technology may actually limit access rather than extend it. Rural areas still suffer from inadequate telecommunications infrastructure (Rural Clearinghouse, 1994). High-income households are much more likely to have access to computers and on-line services than low-income households (Dede, 1994). As access to technology becomes associated with quality of life, those who do not have access will become increasingly disenfranchised from the information-based society.

It would be wrong to give the impression that the open-door mission of the community college, as a goal based on our nation's democratic ideals, has never been questioned (Clark, 1960; Brint and Karabel, 1989). These and other authors contend that the community college has actually reinforced social positioning by tracking most lower-stratum students to certain vocational areas. Their degrees lead them to jobs with little prestige, career advancement, or social mobility.

What role does distance education play in solving social dilemmas of justice, gender, equity and fairness, building community, or equipping students to thrive in the global village? According to Ebben and Kramarae (1993), there is a gender gap on most campuses in terms of access to science and technology information, participation in policymaking forums, and use of computer networks and electronic discussion groups. Clearly, we need to explore the ways in which distance education expands or confines women's roles on campus.

The Telecommunications Act of 1996 will have an impact on the accessibility of telecommunications in three significant ways. In keeping with the trend toward deregulation, the Act allows local and long-distance providers to compete in each other's markets (Salomon and Gray, 1996). The intent of deregulation is to reduce the costs of access by increasing competition and innovation. However, there are also concerns that deregulation of this kind will encourage a rash of buyouts and mergers that may eventually reduce competition. A second important feature of this legislation is that it expands the concept of universal service to include access to advanced telecommunications service at reasonable rates (Salomon and Gray, 1996). It authorizes the Federal Communications Commission to define the services to be included, and, for the first time, considers education as a factor in defining universal service. Telecommunications carriers must offer educational providers and libraries within their service areas reduced rates. Unfortunately, the legislation defines education as limited to K–12, so the potential benefits for higher education are unclear (Salomon and Gray, 1996). Community colleges, working through professional organizations such as the Instructional Telecommunications Council, can become a powerful force in shaping federal telecommunications policy.

Teachers and Teaching

Much of the current thinking about teaching in distance education centers around the view of technology as a force for redefining the work of teaching. However, much of the practical interest in technology is focused upon how technology can be used to support lectures rather than questioning the value of the lecture in the information age (Wilson, 1994). We know the lecture is a reasonably efficient strategy for the transmission of information (Weston and Cranton, 1986). We are also aware that the lecture is a poor method for preparing critical thinkers. Today information is both abundant and quickly outdated. As technology increases our access to huge quantities of information, the challenge is to translate that information into meaningful knowledge.

The question we must begin to ask is how to use technology to help us redefine pedagogy rather than how to use technology to help us prepare better lectures (Wilson, 1994). As information is digitized, it offers opportunities for on-demand learning. Teachers with immediate access to a vast array of learning resources can capitalize upon this, discovering a limitless number of new teachable moments. Telecommunications will enable us to customize learning (Wilson, 1994), provide around-the-clock access to teachers and learning resources (Schweiger, 1994), and shift from teacher-centered to student-centered strategies (League for Innovation, 1993). As the bandwidth capabilities of the telecommunications technologies increase, so will the opportunity to provide richer forms of learning (Wilson, 1994), such as those offered by virtual environments that can better prepare students for real-life experience (Dede, 1991). The on-line environment may increase opportunities for collaborative learning and equalize opportunities by removing many of the social cues that make some learners reluctant to participate in a traditional classroom setting (Harasim, 1990; Kiesler, Siegel, and McGuire, 1984).

However, technology will be effective only if it is used appropriately. While we ask what technology can do, we must also discover what technology will undo (Wilson, 1994). For instance, telecommunications should not be used to reduce the interaction between students and teachers, but to enhance that interaction. Distance education technology will transmit much more information, but may create confusion rather than understanding. All too often, institutions make decisions to adopt telecommunications for reasons of cost-effectiveness rather than learning effectiveness, despite the fact that research indicates that telecommunications does not reduce the costs of teaching (Gunawardena, 1990). It is important that teachers, not technology, be the driving force in the changing pedagogy.

Our current methods of teaching will be difficult to change without substantial changes in the institutional forces that promote the status quo. Specifically, funding patterns, institutional reward systems, and organizational structures work in concert to pull us back rather than to push us forward. Current funding structures designed to measure learning as a function of "time in seat" are increasingly irrelevant to the new pedagogy and become a major barrier to change when effective teaching is defined only by what occurs outside the classroom. In addition, traditional methods of financing capital expenditures are inadequate, often supporting the acquisition of buildings and equipment, with few resources aimed at maintaining, using, and developing infrastructure.

As described by Parisot in Chapter One, the changes teachers must make in adopting the new pedagogy are fraught with risk, but few institutions reward risk taking. Telecommunications teaching, characterized by teamwork, is uncomfortable to teachers accustomed to autonomy. Teachers who use telecommunications find that they must rely on a broader range of support systems than teachers who come to the traditional classroom. Equipment must be functional and reliable, the design of teaching materials often requires assistance, and providing course materials to multiple sites can be problematic. Evaluation instruments are often designed to assess traditional pedagogy, focusing on organization and presentation strategies rather than mentoring and group facilitation skills.

Mission and Boundaries

Bergquist (1993) describes the transition of higher education from a modern to a postmodern era as one shaped by technology. He suggests that in the modern era, colleges and universities were served by well-defined boundaries rather than by well-defined missions. However, in the postmodern era, boundaries are fluid and permeable. In this climate, old questions addressing rules, specialization, and institutional loyalties have little relevance. Our new questions will be conceived in terms of who we are rather than of what we do.

Merging of Institutional Boundaries. Groups of educational institutions working together can help prepare graduates to meet new workforce demands. For example, the National Technological University combines offerings from multiple institutions to offer advanced degrees in engineering at the workplace via satellite. Other collaborative initiatives include the multistate Western Governors University described in Chapter Seven and the Southern Regional Education Board's Electronic Common Market (ECM). The ECM will soon pilot an initiative featuring an electronic catalogue accessible on the Web, as well as the development of multistate agreements designed to facilitate articulation among institutions and states.

Previously viewed as the entry point to college, community colleges are becoming a point of extended learning for students. Community colleges are not only serving as an originator of educational services in their communities, but as a resource linker for communities (MacBrayne, 1995; Holub, 1996). The move toward seamless education described by Spears and Tatroe in Chapter Four will force us to examine long-held assumptions about learning, motivation for learning, who should pay, and who should provide credentials to students.

Community colleges more than any other sector of higher education have developed ties with business and industry. Distance education will strengthen these ties, further bridging the boundaries between higher education and the private sector. In this climate, will the community college mission shift from one of community service to one focused on service to local industry? Will authority over credentialing be shared with the private sector, thus shifting the oversight of education from the public to the private sector? Or will corporations such as GE, IBM, and Xerox—who may find ways to educate their employees more efficiently—threaten higher education's current monopoly over credentialing? (Griffith and Connor, 1994).

Eliminating Geographic Boundaries. Telecommunications technologies make geography increasingly irrelevant. This has ramifications for both community colleges and the communities they serve (Goldstein, 1993). For instance, the community college more than any other sector of higher education has been defined according to geographic service area. These institutions are now being thrust into an environment in which the competition has greater access to their market with neither the costs of maintaining a campus nor the barriers of state regulation.

While states have the authority to regulate institutions within their borders, they do not have the authority to regulate competitors who deliver programs electronically (Chaloux, 1985). Distance education will certainly elevate the tension between the federal government's power over interstate commerce and the states' authority over education. In fact, as distance education eliminates boundaries between state institutions, higher education may become vulnerable to antitrust complaints, since their exclusion in the past has been based upon the assumption that higher education is fragmented (Chaloux, 1985).

As geographic boundaries fade, students will no longer be tied to a location, but can select among a vast array of program offerings. Rossman (1992) envisions a global university in which students take courses from multiple institutions and faculty. Community colleges may soon compete with the major corporations for the best faculty. College teachers may become simply contract employees hired on a course-by-course basis, whose only responsibility is teaching. The authority for oversight of higher education may shift from state to regional control (Jonsen and Johnstone, 1991) or perhaps national control (Schweiger, 1994). The emphasis in oversight may shift from one of regulation to one of consumer protection. The climate of increasing competition may result in increasing pressures to merge, eventually forming large multinational educational institutions.

Conclusion

In the future, colleges will no longer choose between audio or video systems, between interactive or independent systems, or between one-way or two-way systems. A single wire will give us everything and will connect the classroom, the library, the workplace, and the home. The problem will not be a problem of choosing the right system for an institution but of choosing the most practical combination of learning experiences for a particular learning event, based on a trade-off between the costs and capabilities of a vast array of media options. Thus as our instructional options increase so does the number of complex instructional decisions.

In this environment, the focus of our educational organizations will shift from teaching to learning. Adapting to this shift will require educational organizations to adopt new approaches for defining faculty work and funding learning. These shifts will bring fundamental changes in our views about how education is organized, why people learn, and who should pay. The community college of the future may not look much like the community college we know today. In an environment characterized by permeable boundaries and fluid relationships, the community college may no longer be a place but an idea—an idea that represents the development of the human potential, as embodied in its open-door mission. This idea is one that can be invigorated by distance education.

Issac Asimov once said that the thing to predict is not the automobile but the parking problem. This statement touches our apprehension toward technology and its power to change us in ways we do not wish. Some fear technology will debase higher education by making it a strictly economic enterprise. If higher education adopts a head-in-the-sand response to technology, then the "parking problems" will continue to plague us. The community college, as the representative of our vision of educational opportunity for *all,* stands poised to demonstrate how distance education can provide education for each.

References

Bergquist, W. *The Postmodern Organization: Mastering the Art of Irreversible Change.* San Francisco: Jossey-Bass, 1993.

Berman, P., Wyman, R., and Kunz, K.. *The Feasibility of Statewide Distance Education: Commission on Innovation Policy Discussion Paper Number 5.* Berkeley, Calif.: Commission on Innovation, Sept. 1972.

Blanchard, W. *Telecourse Effectiveness: A Research-Review Update.* Olympia: Washington State Board for Community College Education, 1989. (ED 320–554)

Brey, R. *U.S. Postsecondary Distance Learning Programs in the 1990s: A Decade of Growth.* (Report No. JC 920 023). Washington, D.C.: Instructional Telecommunications Consortium, American Association of Community and Junior Colleges, 1991. (ED 340 418)

Brey, R., and Grigsby, C. *A Study of Telecourse Students.* Washington, D.C.: Annenberg/CPB, 1984.

Brint, S., and Karabel, J. *The Diverted Dream.* Boston: Oxford University Press, 1989.

Brock, D. "Research Needs for Adult Learners Via Television." In M. G. Moore (ed.), *Contemporary Issues in American Distance Education.* New York: Pergamon Press, 1990.

Bruning, R., Landis, M., Hoffman, E., and Grosskopf, K. "Perspectives on an Interactive Satellite-Based Japanese Language Course." *American Journal of Distance Education,* 1993, 7 (3), 22–39.

Chaloux, B. *Assessing Long Distance Learning Via Telecommunications: Project ALLTEL.* Denver, Colo.: Council on Postsecondary Accreditation and State Higher Education Executive Officers Association, 1985.

Chu, G., and Schramm, W. *Learning from Television: What the Research Says.* (rev. ed.) Washington, D.C.: Association of Educational Broadcasters, and Stanford University, Institute for Communications Research, 1975.

Clark, B. *The Open Door College: A Case Study.* New York: McGraw-Hill, 1960.

Cookson, P. S. "Research on Learners and Learning in Distance Education: A Review." *American Journal of Distance Education,* 1989, 3 (2), 22–34.

Dede, C. "Emerging Technologies: Impacts on Distance Learning." *Annals of the American Academy of Political and Social Science,* 1991, 514, 146–158.

Dede, C. *The Technologies Driving the National Information Infrastructure: Implications for Distance Education*. Los Alamitos, Calif.: Southwest Regional Laboratory, 1994.

Dille B., and Mezak, M. "Identifying Predictors of High Risk Among Community College Telecourse Students." *American Journal of Distance Education*, 1991, 5 (1), 24–35.

Dillon, C. L. "The Relationship Between Delivery System and Student Success in Technology-Based Distance Education." Proceedings of the Eighteenth ICDE World Conference: The New Learning Environment. University Park: Pennsylvania State University, 1997.

Duning, B. S., Van Kekerix, M. J., and Zaborowski, L. M. *Reaching Learners Through Telecommunications: Management and Leadership Strategies for Higher Education*. San Francisco: Jossey-Bass, 1993.

Ebben, M., and Kramarae, C. "Women and Information Technologies." In M. Ebben and C. Kramarae (eds.), *Women, Information Technology, and Scholarship*. Urbana, Ill: Women, Information Technology and Scholarship Colloquium, Center for Advanced Study, 1993.

Fletcher, J. D. *Effectiveness and Costs of Interactive Videodisc Instruction in Defense Training and Education*. Alexandria, Va.: Institute for Defense Analysis, 1990.

Garrison, D. R. "An Analysis and Evaluation of Audio Teleconferencing to Facilitate Education at a Distance." *American Journal of Distance Education*, 1990, 4 (3), 13–24.

Gibson, C. C. "Toward an Understanding of Academic Self-Concept in Distance Education." *American Journal of Distance Education*, 1996, 10 (1), 23–36.

Gilcher, K., and Johnstone, S. *A Critical Review of the Use of Audio Graphic Conferencing Systems by Selected Educational Institutions*. College Park: International University Consortium, University of Maryland, 1989.

Goldstein, M. B. "Academic Regulation of Telecommuted Learning." *AACC Journal*, 1993, 64 (3), 32–33.

Griffith, M., and Connor, A. *Democracy's Open College*. Portsmouth, N.H.: Boynton/Cook, 1994.

Gunawardena, C. N. "Integrating Telecommunications Systems to Reach Distance Learners." *American Journal of Distance Education*, 1990, 4 (3), 38–46.

Harasim, L. M. "Online Education: An Environment for Collaboration and Intellectual Amplification." In L. M. Harasim (ed.), *Online Education*. New York: Praeger, 1990.

Holmberg, B. *On the Status of Distance Education in the World in the 1980s: A Preliminary Report on the Fern Universitat Comparative Study*. Hagen, West Germany: Zentrales Inst. fur Fernstudienforschung Arbeitsbereich, Fern Universitat, 1985. (ED 268 969)

Holt, D., Petzall, S., and Viljoen, J. "Unleashing the Forces: Face-to-Face Study Groups at a Distance." *Distance Education*, 1990, 11 (1), 125–149.

Holub, J. D. *The Role of the Rural Community College in Rural Community Development*. ERIC Digest EDO-JC-96-02. Los Angeles: ERIC Clearinghouse for Community Colleges, University of California, 1996. (ED 391 558)

Jonsen, R. W., and Johnstone, S. M. "The Future of Information Technology in Higher Education: The State Perspective." *Change*, 1991, 23 (1), 42–46.

Kiesler, S., Siegel, J., and McGuire, T. W. "Social Psychological Aspects of Computer-Mediated Communication. *American Psychologist*, 1984, 39 (10), 1123–1134.

Kulik, C.-L. C., and Kulik, J. A. "Effectiveness of Computer-Based College Teaching: A Meta-Analysis of Findings." *Review of Educational Research*, 1980, 2 (2), 525–544.

Kulik, C.-L. C., and Kulik, J. A. "The Effectiveness of Computer-Based Adult Education: A Meta-Analysis. *AEDS Journal*, 1986, 19 (2–3), 81–108.

League for Innovation in the Community College. *What Presidents Need to Know About the Impact of Networking*. Mission Viejo: League for Innovation in the Community College, Oct. 1993. (ED 367 433)

MacBrayne, P. S. *The Way of the Future for Rural Community Colleges*. New Directions for Community Colleges, no. 90. San Francisco: Jossey-Bass, 1995.

McNeil, B. J., and Nelson, K. R. "Meta-Analysis of Interactive Video Instruction: A 10-Year Review of Achievement Effects." *Journal of Computer-Based Instruction*, 1991, 18 (1), 1–6.

Moore, M., and Kearsley, G. *Distance Education: A Systems View.* Belmont, Calif.: Wadsworth, 1996.

Moore, M., and Thompson, M. "The Effects of Distance Learning: A Summary of the Literature." *ACSDE Research Monograph Number 2.* University Park: Pennsylvania State University, 1990.

Morrison, J. L. "Critical Events Affecting the Future of Community Colleges." *Proceedings of the AACC Presidents Academy Summer Experience.* Breckenridge, Colo., July 9–13, 1995. (ED 384–367)

Nixon, D. E. *Simulteaching: Access to Learning by Means of Interactive Television.* Community/Junior College Quarterly, 1992, *16* (2), 167–175.

Nugent, G. C. "Pictures, Audio and Print: Symbolic Representation and Effect on Learning." *Educational Communications and Technology,* 1982, *30,* (3), 163–174.

Powell, R., Conway, C., and Ross, C. "Effects of Student Predisposing Characteristics on Student Success." *Journal of Distance Education,* 1990, *5* (1), 5–19.

Pugliese, R. R. "Telecourse Persistence and Psychological Variables." *American Journal of Distance Education,* 1994, *8* (3), 22–39.

Rudenstine, N. "The Internet and Education: A Close Fit." *Chronicle of Higher Education,* 1997, *53* (24), A48.

Rossman, P. *The Emerging Worldwide University: Information Age Global Higher Education.* London: Glenwood Press, 1992.

Rural Clearinghouse for Lifelong Education and Development. "Distance Learning Technologies Link Adults to Educational Programming Opportunities." *Rural Clearinghouse Digest,* 1994, *1* (2), 3–8.

Salomon, K., and Gray, T. D. *Implications of the Telecommunications Act of 1996 for Community Colleges.* Washington, D.C.: American Association of Community Colleges, 1996. (ED 391 555)

Schramm, W. "The Researcher and Producer in ETV." *Public Telecommunications Review,* July/Aug. 1977, pp. 11–21.

Schweiger, H. *Open and Distance Learning: Alternative Approaches to the Delivery of Post-Secondary Education.* Minneapolis: Minnesota Higher Education Coordinating Board, 1994.

Tennyson, R. D. "Concept Learning." In T. Plomp and D. E. Ely (eds.), *International Encyclopedia of Educational Technology.* New York: Pergamon Press, 1996.

Tinto, V. *Leaving College: Rethinking the Causes and Cures of Student Attrition.* Chicago: University of Chicago Press, 1993.

Weston, C., and Cranton, P. A. "Selecting Instructional Strategies." *Journal of Higher Education,* 1986, *57* (3), 259–288.

Whittington, N. "Is Instructional Television Educationally Effective? A Research Review." *American Journal of Distance Education,* 1988, *1* (1), 47–57.

Wilson, B. "Technology and Higher Education: In Search of Progress in Human Learning." *Educational Record,* 1994, *75* (3), 9–16.

CONNIE L. DILLON is an associate professor of adult and higher education at the University of Oklahoma, where she specializes in the study of distance education and telecommunications.

ROSA CINTRÓN is an assistant professor of adult and higher education at the University of Oklahoma. She specializes in the study of student personnel services and the American Community College.

INDEX

Access: community college mission of, 73, 93; distance learning and, 73, 95–96; Telecommunications Act and, 96

Accreditation: commissions/associations, 74–80; community college role in, 74, 81–82; guidelines/standards for, 74–80; policy revision and, 74–75; unresolved issues in, 81–82; virtual universities and, 71; Western Governors University and, 71. *See also* Quality assurance, educational

Accreditation guidelines, for distance learning: ACE *Guidlines,* 79–80; Association for Community and Junior Colleges (WASC), 75; Commission on Colleges (NASC), 77–78; Commission on Colleges (SACS), 78; Commission on Higher Education (MSACS), 75–76; Commission on Higher Education (NEASC), 77; Commission on Institutions of Higher Education (NCACS), 77; WICHE *Principles,* 79

Accreditation, distance learning and (study): findings, 74–75; methodology, 74; survey responses, 75–80

Accrediting Commission for Community and Junior Colleges, 75

Acculturation, to change, 9–12

Acknowledgment, need for change and, 7–8, 12

A-e-I-o-u evaluation, 55–56, 61–62

Affirmation, of change, 11–12

Agreement on Guidelines for Classroom Copying, 87

American Association of Community Colleges, 88

American Council on Education (ACE), 75, 79–80

Ansari, M. M., 18, 20

Articulation, distance education and, 71–71

Awareness, need for change and, 8–9, 12

Bennis, W., 20

Benson, G., 35

Bergquist, W., 98

Berman, P, 94, 95

Beudoin, M. F., 17

Blanchard, W., 94

Braskamp, L. A., 9

Brawer, F., 1, 2

Brey, R., 2, 20, 93, 95

Brint, S., 96

Brosk, D., 95

Bruning, R., 95

Bryan, R., 16

Bunting, L. S., 16

Carter, M., 34

CCUMC Fair Access Working Committee, 88

Chaloux, B., 24, 74

Change: acculturation to, 9–12; acknowledgment of need for, 7–8, 12; affirmation of, 11–12; awareness of need for, 8–9, 12; community colleges and, 1, 93; as force in postsecondary education, 5; higher education and, 93; technology as revolutionary, 1. *See also* Innovation; Technological change

Chavkin, N., 34

Chu, G., 94

Clark, B., 96

Clark, T., 16

Clark, T. A., 15, 17

Cohen, A., 1, 2

Coldeway, D. O., 55

Colorado Electronic Community College (CECC), 63, 68

Commission on Higher Education, 75, 76

Commission on Recognition of Postsecondary Accreditation (CORPA), 74

Committee on the Judiciary, 87

Communications Technology Center (Wa.), 70

Community colleges: accreditation and, 74, 80–81; access and, 7, 93; business ties of, 98; change and, 1, 100; changing boundaries of, 98–99; changing mission of, 98; characteristics of future, 23, 100; course delivery of, 69–71; data collection role of, 71; democratization and, 96; distance education and, 93; distance learning partnerships and, 33, 35–42, 69–70; distributed student services and, 66; diversity in, 2; factors

103

and, 94; learner characteristics and, 95. *See also* Accreditation, distance learning and, (study); Accreditation guidelines, for distance learning; Distance education; Distributed learning

Distance learning partnerships: Connecticut example, 34; need for, 33; New Mexico example, 34; New York example, 34–35; Texas example, 34. *See also* Pikes Peak Community College (Colo.) distance learning partnership (case study)

Distance learning technologies: barriers to, 7, 20; low-tech, 45. *See also* Faculty teaching styles, and distance education (study)

Distributed learning: parity in, 80–81; personal interaction and, 95; regional-state tensions and, 81

Distributed student services: community colleges and, 66; Western Governors University and, 66–67. *See also* Student support services

Dively, D., 24

Diversity, 2, 94–95

Dropouts. *See* Retention

Duning, B. S., 17, 18, 19, 20, 95

Ebben, M., 96

Educational policy: accreditation and, 74–75; blueprint for changing, 12–13; community college role in, 31; consensus-building framework for, 12; copyright issues and, 84, 91; distance education and, 15; educational innovation and, 1; financial aid and, 68; role modeling and, 12. *See also* Consensus-building model, for technology-based education; State-level policy, for distance education (study)

Educational Technology and Training Center (Colo.), 70

Educators. *See* Faculty

Electronic publication rights, 85–86

Evaluation, distance education: a-e-I-o-u approach to, 55–56, 61–62; Iowa plan for, 54–57; new dimensions of, 53; stakeholder involvement in, 61; Star School Program indicators and, 57–58

Faculty: anxieties of, 28; compensation of, 27; employment concerns of, 28; role in technological change of, 5

Faculty teaching styles, and distance education (study): discussion, 7–12; findings, 6–7; opinion leaders and, 7; role modeling and, 6, 10, 12; structure, 6; support and, 7, 11; teacher- vs. learner-centered strategies and, 7, 9–10. *See also* Instruction

Faculty-student interaction, 20

Fair use: factors in determining, 87; guidelines for, 87; Internet and, 88–89; policy bodies on, 87

"Fair Use Guidelines for Educational Multi-Media," 84

Feyl, N., 34

Financial aid: distance learners and, 27–28; lifelong learners and, 27; policy changes and, 68; traditional model of, 67; virtual universities and, 67–68. *See also* Student support services

FIPSE/SHEEO project, 23–24. *See also* State-level policy, for distance education (study)

Fletcher, J. D., 94

Florini, B. M., 9

Foster, D., 34

Fund for the Improvement of Post-Secondary Education (FIPSE), 23

Gallagher, L., 24, 30

Garrison, D. R., 54, 95

Gender gap, 96

Gibson, C. C., 95

Gilcher, K., 94

Gillespie, R., 24

Goldstein, M. B., 1, 99

Gray, T. D., 96

Griffith, M., 99

Grigsby, C., 95

Gross, R., 23

Grosskopf, K., 95

Guiding Principles for Distance Learning in a Learning Society, 79–80

Gulliver, K., 24

Gunawardena, C. N., 20, 97

Harasim, L. M., 97

Hart, P. K., 18

Hatfield, D., 24, 30

Higher education: change in, 93; competition and, 1, 99; convention vs. innovation in, 1; copyright policy and, 92; telecommunications in, 1; virtual universities and, 72

Hoffman, E., 95

ORDERING INFORMATION

NEW DIRECTIONS FOR COMMUNITY COLLEGES is a series of paperback books that provides expert assistance to help community colleges meet the challenges of their distinctive and expanding educational mission. Books in the series are published quarterly in Spring, Summer, Fall, and Winter and are available for purchase by subscription and individually.

SUBSCRIPTIONS cost $55.00 for individuals (a savings of 37 percent over single-copy prices) and $98.00 for institutions, agencies, and libraries. Please do not send institutional checks for personal subscriptions. Standing orders are accepted. Prices subject to change. (For subscriptions outside of North America, add $7.00 for shipping via surface mail or $25.00 for air mail. Orders must be prepaid in U.S. dollars by check drawn on a U.S. bank or charged to VISA, MasterCard, or American Express.)

SINGLE COPIES cost $22.00 plus shipping (see below) when payment accompanies order. California, New Jersey, New York, and Washington, D.C., residents please include appropriate sales tax. Canadian residents add GST and any local taxes. Billed orders will be charged shipping and handling. No billed shipments to post office boxes. (Orders from outside North America must be prepaid in U.S. dollars by check drawn on a U.S. bank or charged to VISA, MasterCard, or American Express.)

SHIPPING (SINGLE COPIES ONLY): $30.00 and under, add 5.50; to $50.00 add $6.50; to $75.00, add $7.50; to $100.00, add $9.00; to $150.00, add $10.00.

DISCOUNTS FOR QUANTITY ORDERS are available. Please write to the address below for information.

ALL ORDERS must include either the name of an individual or an official purchase order number. Please submit your order as follows:
   Subscriptions: specify series and year subscription is to begin
   Single copies: include individual title code (such as CC82)

MAIL ORDERS TO:
   Jossey-Bass Publishers
   350 Sansome Street
   San Francisco, California 94104-1342

PHONE subscription or single-copy orders toll-free at (888) 378-2537 or at (415) 433-1767 (toll call).

FAX orders toll-free to (800) 605-2665.

FOR SUBSCRIPTION SALES OUTSIDE OF THE UNITED STATES, contact any international subscription agency or Jossey-Bass directly.